D1588824

BY MOUNTAIN, MOOR AND LOCH

To the Dream Isles of the West.

TO HER

who loved the purple heather and the scream of the whaup on the solitary moor, or by the lone tarn.

BIDEAN NAM BIAN, GLEN COE

" 'Neath the huge crag's frowning rim"

By Mountain, Moor and Loch

To the Dream Isles of the West

By

Thomas Nicol, F.R.S.P.B.

Introduction by

Professor A. D. Peacock, D.Sc., F.R.S.E.

Fifty Illustrations

Eneas Mackay
Stirling

First published 1931

Printed at the Observer Press, Stirling

CONTENTS.

" Where's the coward that would not dare
To fight for such a land."

Marmion.

ILLUSTRATIONS

INTRODUCTION

By A. D. PEACOCK, D.Sc., F.R.S.E.,

Professor of Natural History, University College, Dundee.

MY friend, Mr. Thomas Nicol, has invited me to
write an Introduction to his book. This is a
compliment on two counts—firstly, because it is the
wish of such a lover of Nature as is the author ; and,
secondly, because of the trust it implies, for I have
warned him that I have never written an Introduction
before.

I begin by repaying the author's compliment in
kind—by calling him a " lone wolf " naturalist. The
term may not sound complimentary, and perhaps, too,
does not explain enough to the reader who is
unfamiliar with the ways and words of naturalists.
By a " lone wolf " naturalist is meant one who turns
instinctively to Nature for study, companionship, rest,
solace, joy and inspiration; and one who is indepen-
dent of the academies for these fine things. Here
the metaphor breaks down, for the naturalist I have
in mind returns, whiles, to his fellows and shares his
hard-won treasures with the youngster and the novice.
Such an one is our author.

I have a warm side for this breed for it was one of
them—a small slight man, suffering a thorn in the
flesh, yet with a spirit too great for his frail body—who
opened my eyes to living things. It is often said that
the type is verging on extinction, and, to support the
contention, instances are quoted of the parlous
condition of many Field and Natural History Clubs,
which once possessed real field workers and published

their records, and now are mere struggling lecture societies, living on past glories and parasitic on the good-nature of visiting lecturers. Yet over the whole country there are probably just as many, and more, successful clubs as ever, and certainly there is a more widely-spread and greater appreciation of Nature and the pure and applied aspects of biology. But is the knowledge of living things as deep and first-hand as that which the " lone wolf " gained ? There are many who answer " No," and go on to deplore the college-bred substitute products known as laboratory or bottle biologists. I am not so certain. The " lone wolf " possessed his characteristics because of his nature, and it would be bad biology to believe that a different social environment has so quickly swamped heredity. Indeed, with certain youngsters I have in mind, I am encouraged to assert that the breed more than holds its own. It remains true to type, and is even more lone because many of the so-called Natural History Societies do not encourage the cubs.

None of the above argument applies to our author, as we in Dundee know full well. This book will prove it to a larger public ; for here is spread the rich spoil of years of wandering and questing in a lovely and magic land. It is my privilege to bid you share it with him—and be welcome.

A. D. PEACOCK.

PREFACE.

THIS book is the outcome of the wanderings of many years amongst the wild hills and glens of Scotland.

These wanderings were made partly with a view to the study of wild bird life in the glens and of sea birds amongst the isles of the west, partly for the fascinating sport of mountaineering and of watching the birds of the high peaks in their natural haunts, and partly just for pleasure. It is hoped that the book may be of some interest to lovers of nature and to those who are used to the rucksack and the broad highway, or the lone track through the heather to the grey hillside. It is not in any sense of the word a guidebook ; only a record of personal reminiscences coloured here and there with a touch of imagination. I hope I have been able to convey to the reader, with the assistance of the illustrations, some of the keen joy I have felt in my wanderings in lonesome places, and I have endeavoured to make the spirit of the wild spill over in these pages.

The chapters on the west coast, that incomparable scene of the rarest and wildest beauty, are the result of the ramblings of more years than I care to tell— ramblings which have left deeply enshrined in my heart fond memories of those enchanted isles, where the little thatched homesteads nestle in the hollow, and the peat reek curls up into the breathless sky of a mellow summer evening.

When I wrote the chapters on St. Kilda, although there were rumours in circulation of discontent amongst the people regarding their distress during winter, one scarcely believed they were serious in their request to the Government to be removed from their ancestral home, but events proved that they were. The Under-Secretary of State for Scotland entered into negotiations with the St. Kildans, and, almost before one realised what had happened, they were removed to the mainland, and this romantic Isle is now in the sole possession of the sea birds. I have since then added Chapter XV dealing with the evacuation of the Island.

Some of the chapters may seem familiar to many readers, as in their original form they were given as broadcast " Talks ; " but they have all been expanded and rewritten to suit their present purpose.

My thanks are due to Mrs William Sharp for granting me permission to quote from *Iona*, by Fiona Macleod.

The illustrations throughout are from my own collection, with the exception of a few beautiful photographs kindly lent me by Winifred Wilson. To her I am also deeply indebted for many valuable suggestions and helpful aid, and for her untiring efforts to make my book a success. To Phyllis Shepherd I am also under obligation for placing many invaluable hours at my disposal, and for undertaking the tedious and laborious task of deciphering and typing a very cramped manuscript. But for their generous help this book would never have been published.

THOMAS NICOL.

ELLISLAND, MARYFIELD,
        DUNDEE.

THE BRIG O' TURK.

"*And when the Brig o' Turk was won
The headmost horseman rode alone.*"

TIR-NAN-OG

WINTER is gone—farewell. The cloud wrack breaks
   And sweeps across the leaden western sky;
The breeze comes up, the twittering aspen shakes;
   The regal sun smiles through the clouds on high.

   *   *   *   *   *   *   *   *   *

Far in the western seas there lies an Isle,
   Sport of the waves, lashed with an angry roar;
To-day its peaks are sun-kissed, smiling—while
   Sweet spring brings back the sea birds to its shore.

Thou elfin Isle—the waters moan and sigh
   Among thy caves, Land of Eternal Youth,
Whose cliffs and peaks soar up into the sky;
   Spring ever smiles on thee—oh, land of truth!

   *   *   *   *   *   *   *   *   *

I see thee now, dream Isle, 'mid sparkling seas;
   I hear the water lapping on the shore;
I hear thy call, 'tis whispered down the breeze;
   Enchanted Isle, for thee I sigh once more.

T. N.

B

PROLOGUE.

THE CALL OF THE WILD.

" May the hills lie low,
May the sloughs fill up
In thy way.

May all evil sleep,
May all good awake,
In thy way."

Gaelic Blessing of the Road.

THE breath of spring is in the air, and the warm sun shines out of a blue and cloudless sky. The gaunt, naked branches of the trees are motionless.

Nature has shaken off her dull and dreary mantle and smiles upon the earth again with a kindness that there is no mistaking. The trees are stirred to life and the limes are bursting into tender pale green shoots. Those harbingers of spring, the snowdrop and the crocus, the wood anemone and the modest primrose in the dell, are garlanding the earth with white and mauve and yellow, while the tiny harebell, pride of the glens and lonely places, is nodding its blue head to the lazy, whispering western breeze.

The fairy folk are busy chattering amongst the flowers, discussing other colours in which to paint the glen anew, for the pageantry of summer will soon be on us. Oh yes, the little folk are there, but they are only seen and heard by those who love them!

The swallows, too, have left their home in the far

sunny south, and after their long flight of thousands
of miles over land and sea, will soon be amongst us
again. A poor, bedraggled wanderer, tired and
weary of wing, has just arrived, and with great difficulty has reached its old abode in the ruined castle.
The blackbird and the mavis are uttering some
wild, discordant notes, but their voices will soon be
attuned to that deep, melodious song which fills the
woods and dales with music.

Yes, signs of spring are everywhere !

The burn has lost its dull and wintry gurgle, and
has burst into a cheery tinkle as it wimples down
the glen. The snow has nearly disappeared from
the hills, and it is only in the corries of the higher bens
that long streaks can be seen lying amongst the rocks :
that too will soon disappear, and then summer will
be at our doors.

How glorious that magic word, summer, sounds
to the lover of the moor and the glen, the mountain,
the loch, and the lonely tarn of the hills ! It is like
music in his ear—wild voluptuous music that makes
his blood leap, and he longs again for the fragrant
smell of the bog myrtle and the odour of the old peat
moss.

His memory travels backward to some bygone day
—it may be long ago, but to him it is as yesterday.
Perhaps he sees himself marching along the broad
highway, but it is more likely to be on the mountain
side or in the lone glen : wherever it is, it is a remembrance of ever moving onwards in answer to some
irresistible call.

If it be the lone glen that leads him to the hill,
maybe he will see from its steep slopes the sheen of

silvery water dancing and glistening in the sunlight, and beckoning him on like that mysterious will o' the wisp which dances over the bogs of Rannoch twixt the gloamin' and the mirk. But he knows it is no will o' the wisp. It is the " sea sparkle," and he hears the echo of a soft, sweet voice crooning a Gaelic air far away where the sun is setting in the mystic west. The blue islands are calling there, and he can see and smell the peat reek curling up from the wee thatched roof hidden away amongst the heather. He hears the wild scream of the sea birds and sees their white wings as they circle around their craggy home.

Yes, the call is in the air, he can resist it no longer. So, flinging on the old familiar rucksack, and pulling on his hobnailed boots, he shakes the dust of the city from his feet, and with a stout heart sets out along the highway which leads to the open spaces. Through many a scene of beauty, in which he fain would linger, he is drawn onwards towards the setting sun, along the track which leads him ever to the west.

Does he seek for Tir-nan-Og beyond the sunset ? Will he find the Isle of Dreams, the Land of Heart's Desire ?

CHAPTER I.

THE TROSSACHS.

" So wondrous wild the whole might seem
The scenery of a fairy dream."
Scott.

THERE are few lovers of Scottish scenery who have not seen the Trossachs. But how many have seen its real beauty? The majority of visitors rush through, chiefly now by motor car, our American cousins generally reading a guide book all the time. It were better they had never gone at all, for they only get a confused idea of the place.

The word " Trossachs " means " the bristled country," and the name is generally applied to the vale lying between Loch Vennachar and Loch Katrine ; but I use it here in a general sense, for the whole of the surrounding country may be called the Trossachs, and is justly entitled to this name.

In days gone by it was one of the sights of the far-famed valley to see the stage coaches ranged up in order at the Trossachs pier for the homeward journey, the long procession led by the four-in-hand with the old driver arrayed in all the dignity of his scarlet coat and white hat. With a look over his shoulder to see that all were in readiness he gathered up the " ribbons," and to a crack of his whip out swung the long row of coaches to wend their way slowly through the bracken and heather. The graceful silver birch waved high overhead, as they travelled down a steep and narrow defile leading to the Trossachs glen, and on to the hotel where a halt was always made. Those good old days have gone, never to return, and few now follow on foot the track of the " fiery cross " from Bealach-nam-Bo to St. Bride's chapel at the foot of Ben Ledi.

This is an interesting mountain. Its name signifies the hill of God, and Druidical worship took place there long after it had disappeared elsewhere in Scotland. The view from the top on a clear day is a gigantic panorama. Callander nestles at the foot of the crags, a pretty picture set in a frame of purple heather. Over the top of the Abbey Craig at Stirling you can see the outline of Edinburgh Castle dimly silhouetted against the sky. Towards the north, the land of the mountain and the flood, there is nothing visible but peak after peak, the one more fantastic than the other. Should you be an early riser you may see the sun kindling its flaming beacon and flushing up the topmost peak of Ben Voirlich, while farther north is Ben Lawers, and Schiehallion, the hill of the fairies. Still farther north the rounded summit of Cairngorm and the sharp tooth-like peak of Ben Macdhui appear in sight. Towards the north-west Ben Nevis rears its lofty head to greet you, and near at hand Ben Lomond seems watching with a wary eye the jagged ridges of the " Cobbler " at the head of Loch Long.

Water also adds its attraction. Loch Vennachar, like a long streak of molten lead, lies in front. Behind it is the Lake of Menteith. Towards the right is Loch Achray, and then follows Loch Katrine like a great sheet of burnished silver.

I have been an ardent rambler in my time, and have

LOCH ACHRAY.

" But nearer was the copsewood gray
That waved and wept on Loch Achray."

THE THREE GRACES AND BEN AAN.

" *Ben Aan, heaved high his forehead bare.*"

wandered in many parts, but, though I have seen wilder scenes, I have always come back with the impression that I have never seen anything grander than our own native hills and glens. I have been with them in a wild thunderstorm, in drenching rain, in brilliant sunshine; I have been caught in the mist on the high peaks—and I love them in all their moods.

> Mountain and mist, lone glen and murmuring stream, the shaggy forest, and the grey hillside—these are thy features, Scotland, these the pride of those that love thee.

It has often been the case with popular descriptive poems, that the characters mentioned have, after many years, become living realities. William Tell in Switzerland is a striking instance of this, and so with the characters in *The Lady of the Lake*. Scott has made them real characters; they live and move in the Trossachs, and you will please pardon me if I refer to them as though they were living people. It is interesting to follow the movements of the various characters in the poem, and Scott's descriptions are in many cases so accurate that you have little or no difficulty in doing so. Here and there you may lose the trail where he uses a poet's licence and draws on his imagination, but it is easily picked up again.

The route from Callander to the Trossachs leads out by the old village of Kilmahog, over the bridge that spans the Leny, with the outlying ridges of Ben Ledi on the right, and along the shores of Loch Vennachar, through Lanrick Mead, and on to the Brig o' Turk. It was near the sluices at Loch Vennachar that the fight took place between Roderick Dhu and Fitz James, and Lanrick Mead was the trysting place of Clan Alpine.

> " The muster-place be Lanrick Mead ;
> Instant the time—Speed, Malise, speed."

Then it was at the Brig o' Turk that King James first discovered that he had outstripped all his followers and that he was alone in the chase.

The Brig o' Turk is a great haunt of artists in the summer time, chiefly because of the great beauty of the district around Duncraggan, and the entrance to Glen Finglas.   There are also some very vivid sunsets to be seen there, and at times the rugged face of Ben Venue, with its " crags, knolls and mounds," seems as if bathed in blood.   It is from the Brig o' Turk to Loch Katrine in particular that Sir Walter has woven his web of romance.

The scenery is extremely beautiful along the shores of Loch Achray, with Ben Venue in the foreground. The road is shaded with oak and that well known feature of Highland scenery, the graceful silver birch, and it twines and wends its way along until the Trossachs Hotel is reached.   The original name of the Hotel was Ardcheanacrochan, which means literally, " the high end of the rock."   In the early days it was only an old pendicle which served the needs of travellers passing that way.   It is now an up-to-date hotel where the tourist can have his every demand satisfied.

The Pass of the Trossachs begins a little beyond the hotel, and it was here that King James's horse, " the gallant gray " of the poem, fell.

> " I little thought when first thy rein
> I slacked upon the banks of Seine,
> That Highland eagle e'er should feed
> On thy fleet limbs, my matchless steed !
> Woe worth the chase, woe worth the day,
> That cost thy life, my gallant gray ! "

As you enter the narrow defile and gradually ascend, the scene becomes more and more enchanting. New beauties are disclosed at every step, " where twined the path, in shadow hid, round many a rocky pyramid," and Nature has lavishly bedecked the slopes with wild flowers.

> " Here eglantine embalmed the air,
> Hawthorn and hazel mingled there ;
> The primrose pale and violet flower,
> Found in each cliff a narrow bower;
> Foxglove and nightshade, side by side,
> Emblems of punishment and pride."

In the early days a rocky mound crossed this part and completely barred the way, making it difficult to penetrate farther up the glen. A kind of rude ladder was formed, consisting of creepers and broom growing from the face of the rock, up which one had to ascend to go farther.

About a mile up the pass you suddenly come upon "The Three Graces"—beautiful weeping birches— and looking northwards at this point you get a fine view of the bold bleak outline of Ben Aan. On the other side, Ben Venue rears her head from wooded slopes of mountain ash and pine, and a little farther on Loch Katrine appears in sight arrayed in all her romantic beauty. The loch is serpentine in form, and about ten miles in length. It is very narrow at the Trossachs end, where there is a pretty rustic pier covered with heather. It gradually widens out, however, amidst rocks covered with heath and blae-berry and waving birch and mountain ash.

There is a broad, well-made road running from the

little pier along the north side of the loch. Loch
Katrine, with Lochs Vennachar and Drunkie,
supplies Glasgow with water, and the Corporation
raised the supply in Loch Katrine several feet, thereby
completely demolishing the beautiful " Silver
Strand " where the deer used to come to drink in
the twilight. The Silver Strand ran in a crescent
for a considerable distance out into the loch. I have
walked on this strand, and waded the short distance
between it and the adjacent island. But all is now
gone, and the silver strand is nowhere visible. When
I first visited Loch Katrine many years ago there
was only a narrow track where part of the road is
now. It was then a vale of peace and beauty where
one could wander unmolested.

It was at the Silver Strand that Fitz James, the
Knight of Snowdoun, met Ellen Douglas, and the
beautiful Eilean Molach—Ellen's Isle—lies a little
distance out in the loch from this spot. The island
was used in the early days by the Highlanders as a
place of safety for the women and children when
they were in danger of being attacked. One would
naturally think that the isle derived its name from
the heroine of Scott's poem, but this I believe is not
so. A story is told that when Cromwell's men
reached the Trossachs, the Highlanders, who feared
trouble, removed all their women and children to
the island, and drew up their boats there. They then
took to the hills to await events. One of the soldiers
volunteered to swim across to the island to secure a
boat. Just as he was about to draw himself up on
a jutting rock he was seized by one of the women,
Ellen Stewart, from the Brig o' Turk, who severed

his neck with her *skean dhu*.   And so the island was named Ellen's Isle.

The Pass of Bealach-nam-Bo (the Pass of the Cattle) lies on the opposite side of the loch at the foot of Ben Venue.   Up this pass the cattle were driven for safe keeping after some foray had been made on the Lowlands.   Once in the sheltered ground at the end, and under the care of the *urisk*, who were akin to the brownies and dwelt in the cave beneath the pass, they were quite safe, and there was little chance of their being recovered by their lawful owners.   The easiest way of reaching the opposite side of the loch is to secure a boat at the pier, and row to the pass.   By so doing you get a delightful view of the northern side, and also of Ellen's Isle, where you can land.

It is truly a land of romance and beauty.   I have often lain beneath the trees at the silver strand, and through the blue smoke from my pipe have seen the fair Ellen and the gallant Knight of Snowdoun, Roderick Dhu and Lord Douglas, old Allan-bane and Malcolm Graeme, all passing to and fro in the aisles of imagination.

CHAPTER II.

THE ROB ROY COUNTRY.

"While there's leaves in the forest, and foam on the river,
MacGregor despite them shall flourish for ever."
MacGregor's Gathering.

A LITTLE to the north of the Trossachs lie the historic Braes of Balquhidder, famous for some of the exploits of that bold outlaw, Rob Roy. There is a path which makes a pleasant ramble on a summer day, entering at Duncraggan Huts at the Brig o' Turk and winding through the old deer forest of Glen Finglas to the east end of Loch Voil, which is within a stone's throw of Balquhidder. The glen is steeped in traditional history and vies in beauty with the Pass of the Trossachs. At one part it forms a deep gully, where the roar of the River Turk can be heard, though the river itself is scarcely seen as it tumbles along its rocky bed, or leaps from some jutting rock into the deep pool below. It was in a cave beneath one of these waterfalls that Brian the Hermit went to perform his mystic rites in an endeavour to discover the fate of Clan Alpine in the fight. Tradition tells that, in the days of old, the same cave, just at the foot of the Hero's Targe, sheltered an outlaw, who was fed by some one from above and supplied himself with water by dropping a can attached to a rope into the deep pool below.

Rob Roy and his wife and two sons lie in the graveyard at Balquhidder quite close to the ivy-covered ruins of the quaint old church. When I first visited the old churchyard it was a difficult matter to find the grave, but later the Chief of the Clan erected a strong iron rail, supported on fir cones, around the rough-hewn slabs, with tablets bearing the testimony that Rob and his wife and family lie beneath. The outside slab with a sword carved on it was for a long time pointed out as Rob's grave, but it is now generally understood that his wife, Helen, lies there. The corresponding stone on the other side marks the spot where his two sons, Coll and Robert, lie, while Rob rests beneath the centre slab, which bears a peculiar scroll presumed to be his arms—a fir tree and a sword supporting a crown with a strange looking figure of a child; but the whole has been roughly hewn and is now partially obliterated, so that it is difficult to trace it out. It is said that he claimed relationship with the Royal Stuarts, and this is supposed to be his reason for selecting the crown as part of his arms.

Rob Roy was a successful grazier until he fell into the hands of his enemies, the Duke of Montrose and Graeme of Killearn, who were not slow to take every opportunity of encompassing his downfall. This they meanly and successfully managed during his absence in the north of England, where he had gone to collect outstanding debts to enable him to settle accounts between himself and the Duke, who had entered into a one-sided bargain with him regarding the buying and selling of cattle. Rob was an honest, hard working man until that dreary winter's day when he returned from England prepared to pay his debts, only to find his home demolished and his wife and family wandering outcasts on the wintry hillsides, and he himself unwarrantably proclaimed an outlaw and all his possessions seized. Little wonder then that a man so highly strung should be goaded on through sheer injustice to leave the paths of virtue, and take a solemn oath of vengeance on the threshold of his old home, which now lay in ruins ! Following his outlawry he lived an adventurous career and gathered around him a band of the most daring renegades of his clan, and his name soon became a terror to all who crossed his path. When he got the chance—and the chances were many—he never forgot to deal a deadly blow at his old enemies, the Duke of Montrose and John Graeme, and doubtless these two men regretted the day when they had caused the downfall of Rob Roy. It must be remembered, however, that like Robin Hood of Sherwood Forest, he was ever generous to the poor, and befriended many a helpless widow in distress in those troublous times.

Towards the end of his career the Duke of Argyll arranged a meeting between Montrose and Rob and was successful in bringing about a reconciliation between the two. He ultimately died in peace at Inverlochlarigbeg, Balquhidder, on 28th December, 1734, at the age of seventy-four. While he was on his deathbed, an old enemy, Maclaren of Invernenty, called to enquire for his health, but before he was admitted Rob, as befitted the chief of his clan, insisted on being lifted from his bed and dressed in the Highland garb, with buckler, broadsword and pistols by his side. When the interview was ended he was again lifted into bed and requested that his piper should play *Cha teil, cha teil, cha teil, mi tulidh*, and during the playing of the dirge he died.

ELLEN'S ISLE.

" Here for retreat in dangerous hour
Some Chief had framed a rustic bower."

OLD CHURCHYARD, BALQUHIDDER

" Rob Roy and his wife and two sons lie in the graveyard at Balquhidder quite close to the ivy-covered ruins of the quaint old church."

Some fine specimens of old Highland huts are still in existence on the road between Balquhidder and King's House Inn, and it was no unusual thing to see the smoke pouring out through the cracks in the mud-plastered walls. There is a delightful little bit of wild scenery called the Black Island just over the bridge at Loch Voil, where the Calair burn is divided in two by a mass of huge boulders. One wonders where they have all come from. The stream rushes with great force into the midst of them and instantly vanishes, only to appear again farther on. After forming several beautiful little cascades, the two streams join at the other end of the island and flow on to the River Balvaig, which wends its sluggish course to Loch Lubnaig.

From this point you can walk along the verdant Braes o' Balquhidder to King's House where, should you be tired of tramping, you can hail the engine driver of the first train coming south, when he will pull up and you can go on by train to Callander. Or if you should be inclined for more walking you can turn east at the Black Isle, and take the hill road, from which you will get some delightful views of the surrounding country until you reach Strathyre, where you join the main road down Loch Lubnaig and so through the beautiful Pass of Leny.

To follow some of the exploits of the bold outlaw, the scene shifts from Balquhidder to Aberfoyle, made familiar to every one by Scott's novel, *Rob Roy*.

The moor road from Callander to Aberfoyle is rather dreary until the beautiful Lake of Menteith is reached. It is more circular than other Highland lochs and bears a striking resemblance in some respects

C

to Derwentwater in Cumberland. Parts of its shores are fringed with various kinds of reeds and water lilies, while the southern banks are well wooded, and their shadows reflect far out on the still waters of the lake. There are two islands—Inchmahome (the Isle of Rest) and Talla—the first-named being famous for the ruins of its priory, which was founded by the Earl of Menteith in 1238, and where Queen Mary spent some of her early days. She was carried there for safety after the Battle of Pinkie and remained with her "four Maries" for about nine months. The Priory, consisting of the walls and a handsome Gothic arch, is well preserved and very interesting to the archaeologist. The Isle of Rest must have been a burial ground from an early date and there are some finely carved stones still in existence. There were many very fine old Spanish chestnut trees of enormous girth on the island, but most of them have fallen. The Nuns' walk runs from north to south and practically divides the island, while Queen Mary's bower, a circle of boxwood of enormous height with a thorn tree in the centre, is said to have been planted by the youthful Queen.

Leaving the Lake of Menteith behind we are again in the land of the MacGregor and only a few miles from the " Fords of Frew." Here Rob made one of his most miraculous and daring escapes from the Duke of Montrose who had captured him, and had him bound by a belt to the back of one of the troopers, James Stewart, an old friend of Rob. Stewart never would have taken part in the capture but that, being a tenant of the Duke, he was bound to obey the call. The troopers, led by Montrose, were ordered to cross the river and in so doing Stewart's horse got slightly detached from the others. Rob had been taunting him about taking part in the capture of one who had so often befriended him in his time of need, but Stewart, being afraid of the Duke, was adamant to Rob's wiles. Rob then reminded him that the MacGregors would take swift and dire vengeance on him if anything befell their chief. This had the desired effect, for Rob felt the belt that bound them together slacken so far as to allow him to reach down for the *skean dhu* hidden in his stocking. In a minute the belt was severed and Rob slipped from the back of the horse into the swift running stream where he dived and made for the bank. His movements could scarcely be seen as twilight was falling, and when he rose to breathe he undid his plaid and allowed it to float down with the current, thus deceiving the troopers as to his actual whereabouts. By this time he had reached the northern bank in safety and there were few people in the vicinity who would not help and shelter Gregarach.

The clachan of Aberfoyle lies about five miles from the Lake of Menteith, and its name is familiar to every one because of the scene between Bailie Nicol Jarvie and Major Galbraith in Jean MacAlpine's change house. No such house exists now, of course, but after considerable investigations in the district I came to the conclusion that it might probably have been somewhere about Milton, and, curiously enough, a name-plate has now been placed to this effect opposite the ruins of a fine specimen of a Highland hut there.

Save one or two whitewashed huts on the face of

the hill, and near the road running over to the Trossachs, there are no traces of the old Highland houses now visible. These ancient " bourocks," as they were called in those days, were built of rough stones stuck together with mud, and the roof consisted mainly of rafters of oak and birch, thatched with heather and divots. The walls were very low, and the roofs in some instances almost reached the ground —in fact they seem to have been so low at Aberfoyle that Andrew Fairservice remarked, on seeing them in the morning after his adventure with the Bailie and the Major, that they might have ridden over them in the dark and never been aware, unless their horses' feet had gone through the riggin. It was in the old manse that Sir Walter Scott lived when he was in the district collecting his notes for *Rob Roy*, and the room which he occupied is still carefully preserved.

There is a large garden attached to the manse with a fine old-world flavour about it. There were gilly-flowers in one corner, while the stately holly-hocks adorned another ; and clustered around an old chair, where probably Sir Walter might have sat while pondering over his book, was sweet lavender in great profusion. An ideal place away from the haunts of men where one could sit in solitude, and think, and dream.

The road leading from the manse crosses the infant Forth by an old-fashioned bridge of two arches, very narrow and high in the middle. It was over this bridge that the Bailie and Frank Osbaldistone slowly wandered as the shades of night were falling on the clachan, to keep the appointment made with

PASS OF LENY.

" *A hundred men can hold the pass.*"

Rob in the Tolbooth of Glasgow. If the Bailie could saunter over the bridge to-day he might well exclaim, "ma conscience!" for the ancient "bourocks" of his day have given place to a village of modern villas, and instead of Jean MacAlpine's change house he would be confronted with the spacious Bailie Nicol Jarvie Hotel. He would doubtless recognize the old oak tree that stands in front of it, though he might gaze in wonder and doubt at the " coulter " hanging from a branch, and said to be the poker which served him in good stead on that memorable night when he met Major Galbraith at the inn.

William Glen, the gifted author of *Wae's me for Prince Charlie*, lived in a cottage on the moor near Duchray Castle. The castle was well known to Rob, for several times he had been imprisoned there. When visiting the castle I was shown a dark lobby with a window recess in one corner, and was informed that once, when he was being removed, his jailer was leading the way along this lobby with a lit "cruisie" when Rob suddenly knocked the light out and swung himself out of the window, dropping into the courtyard at the back and making his escape across the river.

Loch Ard is one of our most beautiful lochs and is almost divided in three by " the Narrows," two smaller lochs at the lower end, the larger being at the upper end. It is bold and rocky at some parts and beautifully fringed with a mass of water lilies and bulrushes. It is from the water that its bold and picturesque beauty can best be appreciated, and when you emerge from the second loch the pass

on the right immediately arrests your attention.
Towards the upper end and just where the road
vanishes in the wood is the marvellous echo rock—
I have heard my own voice distinctly repeated four
times. On the opposite side of the loch the scenery
is wild and rocky, with a deep cave frequented by
Rob when he was badly wanted elsewhere.

The famous Liddard Falls and Punchbowl are
near the top of the loch, and it was there that Waverley
and Flora Maciver met in Scott's *Waverley*.

There are many interesting by-roads in the
vicinity, and one in particular—a bridle path—leaves
the highway at Stonefield, just at the end of the golf
course, skirts the base of the Menteith hills, and
ultimately brings you out at the east end of Loch
Vennachar. The scenery is delightful all the way
but there are few landmarks to guide you, and as the
track is a moorland one, it is a simple matter to lose
it, and unless you are in the possession of a good
compass you may have to cool your blood amongst
the heather for a night.

The district is rich in fairy lore, and there is a
rounded eminence rising to a considerable height and
densely covered with trees known as " The Fairy
Knowe." The Reverend Robert Kirke, once minister
at Balquhidder, and author of a book on fairies,
who seems to have been strangely familiar with all
their ways, while walking on the knowe one day is
said to have been spirited away by the " wee folks,"
probably for having revealed too many of their
secrets. I have explored the Fairy Knowe with
difficulty for the trees are so closely planted and the

undergrowth so dense that one had almost to creep at some parts, but I cannot conscientiously say that I saw or heard any of the little people, otherwise I might never have been able to write this chapter.

CHAPTER III.

KILLIN OF THE MOUNTAINS.

" My heart's in the Highlands wherever I go."—*Burns*.

HAVE you ever noticed how a river has the making or marring of many a Highland clachan? Should the river be slow and sluggish it adds no charm to the village, and its beauty is gone, but should it be a clear, bustling pebbly stream rushing over rocks in a restless hurry, then it adds a picturesqueness to the scene which it otherwise would not possess.

Had Killin been situated a mile or two farther west, where the Dochart flows on silently through its mossy bed, it might never have been heard of as a beauty spot; but just before the river reaches the village it suddenly becomes all life. Rushing through a long succession of rapids, swirling, twisting and heaving itself into the air in a mad frenzy, it divides in two at the Island of Garbhinish. Both parts continue their wild career over a series of long, shelving jutting rocks before they again unite at the other end of the island, where they hurl themselves with terrific force under the old bridge into the deep linn below. Thus has the river Dochart immortalized Killin as one of the beauty spots of the Perthshire Highlands.

Should you enter Killin for the first time from the west, you are lucky. As you wander down the old road leading from Lix toll, the first thing that arrests attention as you draw near the village on the high

RUINS OF PRIORY, INCHMAHOME.

"The Isle of Rest."

Supposed Site of Jean MacAlpine's Change House.

ground is the memorial to the men who fell in the Great War. It is a strikingly realistic piece of work. On the top of a great rough-hewn square pedestal stands a Highlander with that grim look we knew so well in those terrible days. He is looking across the moor with the great silent hills around him. All the crevices in the rough blocks are filled in with wild flowers and small ferns gathered on the mountains, while around the borders of the pedestal blooms his native heather. The little walk that encircles the memorial is inlaid with white pebbles from the Dochart hard by, while along the front of the walk, inlaid with black pebbles, are the words, " Lest we forget." I have seen many war memorials in various parts of the country, but this one is outstanding from all others and is completely in harmony with its surroundings.

A little below the memorial you get your first peep of Killin, a row of picturesque, whitewashed, thatched cottages leading down to the old bridge. Across the bridge is another row of thatched cottages, and beyond that the village is quite modern, and consequently loses the charm and beauty which the upper end possesses.

There are always passers-by lingering on that bridge. Do you wonder at it ? The scene is quite Alpine in appearance. Up the western valley is the river rushing and roaring around the island, which is covered with wind-swept old pines. There are many of these old pine trees in the district, said to be relics of the old Caledonian forest. The steep slopes of Stronachlachan rise abruptly on the right. On the left the long purple stretches of moorland rise in gradual slopes, ever upward. The white quartz patches on the top of Beinn Leathan gleam in the sunshine, while in the background of the picture is to be seen the tall cone of dark Ben More, flanked by the far-flung ridges of Stobinian, running down into Inverlochlarig glen near the head of Loch Doine.

Turning to the other side of the bridge we find that the river is again divided in two by the sacred Isle of Inch Buie, which was the burial ground of the ancient Clan MacNab. They were a stalwart race, those MacNabs of the early days, and great clan fighters. Their motto was a characteristic one— " Dreadnought "—and their badge a sprig of heather. They owned all the land as far as the eye could reach, and were lavishly hospitable and careless and regardless of the morrow, with the result that they fell on grievous days, and ultimately their lands were bought by Breadalbane. The greater portion of the clan emigrated to Canada, where they made some name for themselves, especially as fighters. The sacred isle is a quaint old place, delicately carpeted with pale yellow moss, from which it takes its name, and with the exception of a space in the centre, where the burial ground is, it is overgrown with tall gnarled pine trees. They almost encircle you and meet overhead, and on a hot summer day it is so shaded and cool and shut out from the rude world that you feel— here at last lies in peace a turbulent clan, with the stock dove and the stream murmuring their requiem over the dead.

Looking down stream from the bridge you are confronted with the massive form of Ben Ghlas, with the highest ridge of Ben Lawers just peeping over the top.

The church attracts attention by its Alpine appearance. It is quite a plain building inside, but it has a magnificent stained glass window which was designed and made in Munich for Taymouth Castle, and was ultimately presented by the Marquis to Killin. The church was built in 1744, and for age it cannot compare with the venerable sycamore tree alongside, which is said to be three hundred years old, and which is used as the village bill-posting station. If that tree could speak it would quote the words of Hamlet, " To what base uses may we not come, Horatio."

From the top of Stronachlachan a fine view of the whole countryside is to be had. It is rather a steep climb at first, but when you reach the remains of an old road you can follow it and zigzag the hill if you do not care for the steeper climb. The village lies nestling at your feet just like a toy village amongst toy trees, it all seems so tiny, neat and clean from this height—for you are nearly two thousand feet up at this point. On the south all the peaks are distinctly clear, from Glen Ogle, the Scottish Kyber Pass, to Ben More. In front lie the long serrated ridges of Creag-nan-Cuilliach, Meall-nan-Tarmachan, Ben Ghlas and Ben Lawers, while at their feet lies Loch Tay like a narrow strip of blue ribbon. You can drop down over the back of the hill into Glen Lochay, where an old wooden bridge crosses the river a little below the falls, which are one of the many delights of the glen. The river narrows between the steep grey rocks above the falls, and hurls itself with terrific force over a succession of rapids with leaps and bounds into the deep pool below, where the spray rises in dense clouds. When the sunshine, severed into long slanting shafts by the dense pine trees all around, is focussed on the spray, a succession of beautiful rainbows can be seen spanning the narrow glen.

You can take the highway back by the old Lochay Inn to the village about three miles distant. The road runs along the steep slopes of Creag-nan-Cuilliach, which are densely wooded at this part, and the glen is completely shut in on both sides until you reach the little whitewashed inn at the junction with the main highway. Keep a sharp lookout while walking along the road, for the golden eagle frequents some of the high peaks in the glen, and if your luck is in you may get a glimpse of the king of birds as he circles high overhead.

Across the old wooden bridge that spans the Lochay, and at the end of that wonderful avenue of ancient lime trees, stand the ruins of Finlarig Castle, once the seat of the Breadalbane family. Grim deeds of a long forgotten past are written large over the hoary old walls. It has a dungeon where numberless crimes were committed, and a window where they used to sit and watch the poor wretches dangling from the hanging tree. It is an eerie place yet, Finlarig, especially when the darkness falls, or a crescent moon dimly shines through the filmy haze of a summer night. I have often stood beneath the gnarled old oaks and sycamores that surround the crumbling walls just before the " witching hour," and listened to the strange noises of the night and to the hooting of the owls that haunt the ruins. The long-drawn-

LOCH TAY.

"From the top of Stronachlachan, Loch Tay lies at their feet like a narrow strip of blue ribbon."

out hoot of the tawny owl, and the wild shrieks of
the barn owl suggest to an imaginative mind the wailing
of the departed spirits that probably still haunt the
place. One had the dread that from a deep recess
or shady nook might spring a clansman in tattered
tartan, with drawn claymore ready to avenge some
dark crime committed in the unwritten past—but let
us leave the gloom of Finlarig behind, and get out into
the sunshine again.

One of the great attractions of Killin is Loch Tay,
where a little steamer plies daily between Killin and
Kenmore. Although the loch is not to be compared
with Loch Lomond, Loch Awe or Loch Katrine, the
sail is a very delightful one, and the scenery is very
pretty on leaving Kenmore, and again on arriving
at Killin Pier.

The best views of the district are to be had from
Ardeonaig, whence a track leads over the hills to
Comrie and Crieff. There you have an uninterrupted
view of the loch both east and west. In front, the
massive proportions of Ben Lawers are best seen,
while westward the view is magnificent. From the
main road on the opposite side of the loch, both
Creag-nan-Cuilliach and Meall-nan-Tarmachan are
dwarfed by the amount of moorland and high ground
in front, while the top of Ben Lawers itself is scarcely
ever visible; but at Ardeonaig the rugged ridges
of Cuilliach and Tarmachan towering up into the sky
have quite an Alpine appearance.

The ascent of Ben Lawers is not a difficult one,
and the view from the cairn is grand. The track begins at Lawers Inn, up the side of the stream as far
as the road leads, then, turning to the left, the ascent

is gradual until you pass the lonely tarn of Loch-na-Chat where the real climb begins, and it is very steep from there up to the cairn. It is not, however, the view from the top that has made Ben Lawers so well known, but the fact that it has become world-famous as the Mecca of collectors of rare Alpine plants. The rarest of our saxifrages are to be found on the top, and one of the rarest British ferns, the little *Woodsia Hyberboria* is to be found on the inaccessible cliffs overhanging Loch-na-Chat.

There are endless delightful rambles around Killin, and those who love the mountains will find Ben Lawers, Creag-nan-Cuilliach, Beinn Leathan, Beinn Chaluim, Ben More and Ben Voirlich all within easy reach.

CHAPTER IV.

WILD NATURE IN GLEN LYON.

"Where the hazel bank is steepest
Where the shadow falls the deepest."
Hogg.

FORTINGAL, with its hotel and cluster of neat little thatched cottages covered with creepers and rambler roses, is the nearest place to Glen Lyon. It is one of the most charming villages in the Perthshire Highlands, but might have been little known had it not been for its remarkable yew tree. It stands in a corner of the old churchyard surrounded by a wall, and its aged limbs are supported on stone buttresses. It is said to be the oldest tree in Europe, but its actual age seems to be quite lost in the dim mists of antiquity. The girth of the tree, before it was destroyed by people kindling their " Beltein " at its roots, was fifty-two feet. This habit of kindling " Beltein " was nothing short of an old form of fireworship. Both in the north and south of Scotland the beginning of summer was known as " Beltein." At that time, in the days of the Druids, every fire was extinguished and no one dared light them again until " the sacred fire of peace " was obtained direct from the Druid priests.

Glen Lyon, about a mile from Fortingal, is nearly thirty miles long, and is the narrowest, the gloomiest in winter, and one of the grandest glens in Scotland ; in fact it possesses features of all the others in one.

To see a snowstorm in mid-winter at the mouth of the glen is a sight never to be forgotten. The wind rushes in from every direction, and the snow flakes are whirled hither and thither until the place is converted into a veritable fairyland. It is so narrow at some parts that in midwinter on a dull day the light never reaches to the river below.

In summer, however, the scene is completely changed, and well do I remember that glorious afternoon when I first penetrated into its depths. The air was full of the hum of honey-laden bees and each little feathered songster was piping his own particular song, while a blackbird and thrush in open competition were pouring forth some mellow notes from the topmost twigs of a tall and stately larch tree. Away high up on the right the slopes of Ben Dearg were covered with purple heather ; soft, fleecy clouds flitted across the sky, and their ever-changing shadows, creeping across the mountain slopes, dyed the heath a deeper hue. Towering over all like a giant sentinel was the dark frowning peak of Craig Mhor rising to a height of 3200 feet.

The entrance to the glen, known as the Pass of Glen Lyon, has a most commanding aspect. The road, which is high up the side of the pass, has been cut out of the solid rock and is protected on the left by a strong wall. The cliffs on the right are covered with creepers of every colour shaded by the birch and mountain ash, which grows out of fissures where the rock has split into fantastic shapes. The moisture collected high above forms itself into tiny rivulets and throws a fairy-like spray over the wild flowers growing in profusion beneath. Below on the left the

PASS OF GLEN LYON.

"*The narrowest, the gloomiest in winter, and one of the grandest glens in Scotland.*"

MacGregor's Leap, Glen Lyon.

" The leap is by no means impossible, especially for
a man whose life is at stake."

gorge is of the wildest description, as if the mountain side had been rent asunder by some mighty upheaval in earlier days. You can hear the roar of the river as it rushes along its rocky bed, but it is often lost to sight in the dark recesses of the glen below. Here and there a mass of gleaming white can be seen as it dashes itself into spray amongst the boulders which have broken loose from the mountain side and form a barrier to its course.

Down the slopes of this gorge, hanging in many cases beyond reach, the graceful *Polypodium vulgare* spreads out its marvellous fronds. I had never seen such lengths of fronds in its natural state before : they were quite exotic in appearance. It grew in a fringe of soft moss starred with countless anemones and there it was continually sprayed from a splashing cascade above. All over the glen and in the deep recesses of the corries on the mountain side are to be found a great many varieties of ferns, but I searched in vain for the *Osmunda Regalis*.

A hundred yards or so farther up the glen two enormous fir trees on either side of the roadway mark " MacGregor's Leap," the spot where tradition says that a MacGregor, being hotly pursued by four bloodhounds belonging to the Campbells, rushed to a projecting ledge of rock on the Lyon and leapt across the river to the rocks on the opposite side. Turning round with drawn dirk, he killed two of the hounds when they leapt across, the third fell into the river and was drowned, while the fourth refused to try the leap. The leap is by no means impossible, especially to a man whose life is at stake, though I should not like to fall amongst the rocks on the opposite side.

D

The glen at this point is of extreme historical interest, and was the scene of a great many doughty deeds. It is recorded that once the MacGregors, being gradually overpowered and finding that their kilts were hampering them in the fight, threw them off and charged with renewed vigour into the foe. The whole glen from beginning to end is steeped in history and romance, and abounds in legendary lore.

The glen gradually widens out into a sylvan valley beautifully wooded with Spanish chestnut, fir, oak and mountain ash. Again it narrows until there is only room for the road and river between the sloping hillsides. The Lyon at this point rushes with great fury through its rocky channel, and when you peep down through the green foliage bordering its banks there is nothing visible but masses of spray and white water dashing hither and thither. The slopes are thickly carpeted with green moss which makes a delightful background for the pale blue of the delicate little harebell, the dazzling yellow of the bedstraw and St. John's wort, the purple of the wild geranium, and the delicate white of the stately marguerite and stitchwort.

There are some very picturesque waterfalls in the many ravines that intersect the glen, and one of the finest of these can be seen from the road as you pass along. It is spanned in front by an old Roman bridge, but you have to ford the river before you can reach it. I was not the least surprised after getting across to find that it was a haunt of the dipper or water ousel, and apparently the nesting sites were holes in the rocks inside the waterfall—a very secure place and one the dipper is fond of selecting.

The only hamlet in the glen is Bridge of Balgie, where there is a post office, and a schoolhouse which serves a very wide district. Just above the bridge an avenue of trees of great age, chiefly beeches and limes, leads up to the fine old Castle of Meggernie, which dates back to 1582, and contains some excellent specimens of tapestry work. There are also a number of great larch trees near the garden, which it is said were the first to be introduced into Scotland. Beyond this the road is rather rough and the glen is little known, but it still winds on for a considerable number of miles till it reaches Loch Lyon, where the road ends. A bridle path, however, continues westward through the mountains, turning down the watershed of Ben Douran, and ultimately reaches the main road about midway between Bridge of Orchy and Tyndrum.

The glen is a happy hunting ground for the naturalist. Little brown squirrels are constantly crossing the path, while overhead they keep up a series of gymnastics, leaping from tree to tree. Now and then they will stop, and flattening themselves out on a branch above your head, lie still for some time carefully watching you with their sharp, beady eyes.

While sitting on the stump of a tree which commanded a wide stretch of country I suddenly caught sight of a number of small brown objects moving slowly along the opposite hillside. I immediately adjusted my binoculars and discovered that what I had seen was a fine herd of deer, led by a magnificent stag. I watched them carefully for a long time, as they stopped to nibble at the grass, then moved slowly on again. They had almost reached the summit when the stag suddenly stopped and tossed his antlered head in the air, apparently scenting danger in the wind. He stood in this graceful attitude for some little time while the others continued peacefully grazing. At last, the tainted breeze convinced him that danger was near, so he trotted up the slope followed by the others and disappeared over the brow of the hill.

Now here let me say a word on behalf of the field glass. If you have one never go to the country without it, and if you are the happy possessor of a prism binocular, then you have a friend indeed. It is most interesting to lie in a wood, watching the birds and animals around, for they will come quite close if you keep perfectly still. It is, however, when they are at some little distance that the binocular proves your best friend. While watching the deer on the opposite hillside my glass seemed to bring them within a few yards of me, and so I had the delightful privilege of watching their every natural movement.

On consulting my watch I found that it was time to retrace my steps. The shades of night were beginning to fall, and all nature seemed to be assuming a sombre hue. Long, slanting shadows fell across the path. The high mountain peaks were bathed in a dull blue colour, and faint traces of golden streamers shooting up into the sky indicated where the sun was setting. The evening air was redolent of sweet-scented myrtle and wild thyme. Blue tits, linnets and little willow wrens were still calling in the bush, and a thrush was pouring forth his evensong from a

tree on the hillside. The far-reaching call of a
curlew could be heard up the slopes of dark Craig
Mhor—a sound that seemed to be peculiarly in harmony with its surroundings, for wherever the scream
of the curlew is heard you are sure to be in close
touch with wildest nature. Blackcocks kept
constantly uttering their guttural notes, as they
whirred over my head, and the wail of a belated
lapwing, calling to his mate, just faintly reached me
from the Roman camp on the plain below.

On rounding a bend in the road I was startled by
the shrill call of a bird apparently in distress. The
sounds were coming from a large oak, and on
cautiously investigating the cause I found that a
sparrow hawk, apparently in need of an evening meal,
was trying conclusions with a blackbird. The fight
seemed to be very evenly contested so long as they
remained in the tree, but the blackbird made the
great mistake of flying into the open. The hawk,
swift as an arrow, rose into the air, and prepared to
swoop down on its quarry. Down it came like a
bolt from the blue and struck home. There was
a shower of feathers, and both birds dropped heavily
to the ground. The hawk had distinctly the better of
the round, and fearing that it soon would be all over
with my black friend, as he seemed undoubtedly
the worse of the fall, I thought it time to interfere,
so ran in and ended the fight. The poor blackbird
crept into some scrub wood near by, uttering inarticu-
late sounds as he disappeared ; doubtless they were
meant for thanks for my timely help. The sparrow
hawk had meantime taken up his abode on the branch
of a tree, and viewed me with anything but a friendly

eye.   I shook my fist at him as I passed along, when he instantly left his perch and with a parting screech of contempt betook himself into the shadowy recesses of the glen.

Once more I was through the pass, and a brisk walk of a quarter of an hour brought me back to Fortingal. When I reached the village the shades of twilight had given way to darkness, and as I stood and listened for a few minutes in the dim solitude of the night all nature was hushed and had gone to rest. There was no sound save the gentle rustle of the wind in the trees, and on some distant hillside the hooting of an owl, " the tuneless bird of night."   Darkness had fallen on Glen Lyon.

CHAPTER V.

RAMBLES ROUND PITLOCHRY.

" The long light shakes across the lake
And the wild cataract leaps in glory."

Tennyson.

HIGHLAND scenery acts like a magnet to most people, for once you have come within its influence, its charm cannot be resisted. This is particularly so with the district around Pitlochry, which is a name familiar to everybody, and at Fisher's Hotel they are proud to show you in the visitors' book a long list of distinguished names.

The district is rich in flora and fauna, and a day's rambling on the river banks, or hills, or moors, has been productive of specimens of nearly two hundred different kinds of wild flowers and ferns. I do not know of any great rarity in wild birds having been discovered, but there is a great variety of all kinds. I have often watched the oyster catchers on the river, and in spring the cuckoo is heard. Gray wagtails are also numerous, and one day I counted eight curlews close to the village.

Pitlochry lies in the midst of an amphitheatre of hills and the climate is therefore very mild; in warm weather one is glad to climb to the top of Craigour to feel a cooling breeze. The scenery is not as wild as is to be found in other parts of the Highlands, but it is very pleasing, with its alternation of straths, hills, and dales. The hills are picturesque, being mostly wooded with oak and silver birch, and here and there a rough peak rises ablaze with purple heather.

There are some beautiful walks around the district, and Nature has been lavish in her adornment of some of them. The path to the Black Spout, entering at the quarry, winds in serpentine fashion through scrubby pine and blaeberry up the face of the hill, and every here and there glimpses of the strath are to be had. The path gradually narrows, the slopes steepen as you enter the narrow glen, and the stream can be seen far below as it rushes along. You suddenly round a narrow curve, and the beautiful cascade presents itself like a picture. It is a small stream, the Edradour water, but when in full flood it is very effective. High above your head—somewhere about ninety feet—it rushes over a little rocky ledge, where the constant run of the water has made a groove in the rock which sends it out like a spout of white spray, making a striking contrast to the black gloom of the rocks all around.

The path at the west end of the village, leading past the loch to Moulin, makes a cool retreat after the sun of a hot summer day has sunk behind the hills. There are plenty of seats around the loch, and if you feel so inclined it is very pleasant to sit and enjoy a pipe or cigarette with the shades falling fast on Ben-y-Vrackie, and the dim grey twilight intensified by the shadow of the black wood settling down on the water. There is the constant plash of the fish too as they leap after flies, and the sharp call of the coots and moorhens among the long reeds which grow thick around the banks.

The road to the falls of Tummel about three miles

In the Pass of Killiecrankie.

OLD BRIDGE OF GARRY, KILLIECRANKIE.

" Doon by the Tummel and banks of the Garry
Saw ye the lads with the bonnets and white cockades ? "

distant leads over the Cluny Bridge, and along the west bank of the river. Some fine views of the surrounding district are to be had as you pass along. For about two miles the road runs through an avenue of oak and birch along the river side, where the roar of the Tummel at times is deafening. As you emerge from the wood into a beautiful grassy glade, with the picturesque Giant's Steps on the left, the Garry appears in sight and joins the Tummel.

Just beyond the union of the two rivers the noise of the falls can be heard, and as the road approaches the fringe of wood, through the oak and birch can be seen the dark brown water dashing over the rocks. The falls look much better at a distance than on close inspection, as the height, some nineteen or twenty feet, seems greatly to diminish with such a body of water. A far finer sight than the falls, should you not be troubled with giddiness, is to be had if you get as far out as possible on the projecting ledges of rock and look up the river to the bend. There it forms into a succession of rapids, broken every here and there by some hidden rock, and surges and hurls itself about in great dark heaps crested with white foam and spray. I have often watched the salmon pitting their strength against the forces of Nature in a vain attempt to reach the top of the falls, but I have never seen one succeed in doing so. A ladder has now been cut through the rocks on the opposite bank so as to enable them to gain the upper reaches of the river.

The ruins of the old farmhouse of Coillie Bhrochain lie amongst the trees on the opposite side. It derives its name from King Robert the Bruce, who halted there after the Battle of Methven. He was weary and hungry when he arrived at night. The " bhrochain" (brose) was set on the table, of which the King partook heartily, and he named the place Coillie Bhrochain—the wood of the brose.

If you continue your ramble along the road on the left bank of the river you can cross the Tummel at the ferry, a distance of about four miles. To the right a narrow path leads up to a little wooded patch, on crossing which " The Queen's View " of Loch Tummel, a most charming panorama of Highland scenery, lies at your feet. The rock from which the view is obtained is very high, although as it is almost on a level with the road behind, its height is best seen from the opposite bank of the river. At this point, sky, mountain, moor and water all combine in a grand effort to make up one of the loveliest scenes that the eye can look upon.

In the valley below is the Tummel just as it has left the loch, and before it has commenced its head-long rush to disturb the sleepy Tay; on either side the gradual slope of the wooded heights blushing on every peak with purple heather. Over the top of the hills on the south, Faragon has just succeeded in raising its rugged head high enough to catch a peep of the magic scene, while farther west, and towering in proud disdain over all, is Schiehallion, the enchanted hill of the fairies. To complete the scene Nature has laid her mirror in the centre, which catches up and reflects again a magnificent transformation of what has just been described.

Killiecrankie, like Pitlochry, is a name familiar to

everyone. To explore the pass thoroughly you must spend days in it.

If you stand on the old Garry Bridge and look up the stream you will recognize a photograph you have so often seen, but the photograph in this case does not do justice to the original, as the view is one that must be seen. There is the beautiful glen with its steeply wooded slopes stretching on either side—the Garry roaring and rushing down in front, while the dim outline of Ben-y-Gloe, silhouetted like a pyramid against the sky, fills up the background of the picture.

On entering the pass the path leads along the face of the glen on the east side. The west side is very steep and is beautifully wooded with pine and ash, relieved at intervals with graceful silver birch. Every here and there a dark little ravine can be picked out, but it is mainly by the noise of the stream as it dashes itself against the rocks that you know it is there, as the banks are so closely wooded that you can scarcely see it. About midway between the entrance and the "Leap" is the "Soldier's Well," a cool spring of water, where one of Mackay's men was shot from the opposite bank while slaking his thirst after the battle.

A little farther up the pass and just beyond the viaduct is the Soldier's Leap. Tradition says that a Highlander, who had deserted from his side and joined the Lowland ranks some time before, saved his life on the day of the battle by leaping to the other side of the stream when he was hotly pursued by one of Dundee's men. After steadying himself on the rocks below he drew his claymore and dared his pursuer to follow. While standing on the rock with the great dark pool swirling below, and considering the distance from point to point, one is inclined to be sceptical about the story, but of course we must not examine too minutely what tradition says, otherwise the romance of many a fine Highland glen would be gone. I have also been told that a considerable number of years ago the feat was accomplished, and for no other reason than to show that it could be done.

The famous battle was fought at the top of the pass in 1689, somewhere in the immediate vicinity of Urrard House. The battlefield is pointed out by many as much farther to the east, where there is a large stone about six feet high, set down on some maps as " Claverhouse's stone." This, however, from historical accounts of the fight could scarcely have been the actual site of the field, and it seems to have been somewhere near the old mansion house that Viscount Dundee fell. There is a legend told, and believed at Urrard House, that while his horse was drinking at a spring he received his death wound from a bullet fired by one of his own party from a window in the house to avenge some love affair. On a visit to Urrard House once, I was shown this spring, also a beautiful circular mound adjoining, and surrounded by a neatly trimmed hedge, which was said to mark the spot where he died.

The Pass of Killiecrankie has charms peculiarly its own at all seasons of the year. In spring, just after dormant Nature has roused herself, and the bleaker aspect of the fast-fading winter has disappeared, the trees begin to assume their delicate tints of green and from each shady bower the birds charm the air with their first songs. Everything comes early in the pass, for I have been on the road when Ben-y-Gloe was still held hard in the grip of winter and the wind was keen and cutting, but down in the pass it was warm and breathless. In summer, when the air is hot and the sun beats down, it is pleasant to meander along the path under the shade of the leafy trees, or sit by some pool and watch the salmon make a headlong plunge. In autumn a great transformation takes place—and the green gives way to multi-coloured tints, the orange, the browns, and the reds. In winter, when the snow comes down and King Frost reigns supreme, when the fairies begin to play their pranks on the rocks, the stream and the trees—then the whole scene is again changed to a picture of delicate beauty. The powdery snow is dusted thickly over the glen, from tree tops and rocks hang long tapering icicles ; even the stream has muffled its roar under a coating of ice and only its faint murmur can be heard.

And so we ring down the curtain on the glorious pageant of the seasons as seen in the Pass of Killie-crankie.

CHAPTER VI.

AMONGST THE PEAKS OF BEN CRUACHAN.

" Give me the peak where the snowflake reposes."
Byron.

ONE autumn morning I set off from Taynuilt to climb Ben Cruachan, one of the highest mountains of Argyllshire, and one from which a view is obtained which surpasses in extent and beauty that from many a higher mountain. It is one of the finest and most interesting of our many Scottish ranges. Its ridges and the rock face descending into Glen Noe afford good sport to the mountaineer, while the geologist and ornithologist can spend a profitable time wandering amongst its many corries and peaks.

Just after leaving Taynuilt, where the road ascends to the high ground, a distant view is to be had of the entrance to Glen Etive. Although mist was still enshrouding the glen Ben Starav was partially clear, and little wisps of cloud were hanging around the peaks of the Shepherds up at Glencoe. A heavy dew had fallen during the night, and as I entered the woods above Inverawe the first streaks of sunshine glinted along the landscape, and made the lady ferns sparkle as if myriads of diamonds clung to their graceful fronds. The river was in full spate as I crossed the old Bridge of Awe, and was rushing on its headlong course towards Loch Etive. The bridge at one time was the habitat of the little wall rue fern, but workmen had been repairing the struc-

ture, and, so far as I could see, there were very few
ferns left.

The highest peak of Ben Cruachan is a little over
three miles from the main road, but it is a steep climb
all the way, and the last mile is over a mass of huge
boulders and broken rock. The easiest way to
ascend the mountain from the Taynuilt side is to
leave the main road at the Bridge of Awe, taking the
side road to the left, and striking the first ridge just
above the little cottage. This route, however,
necessitates the crossing of the Allt Cruiniche which
runs deep in its rocky channel, and unless you get
over the stream at a high altitude the crossing is
troublesome. To avoid this I kept on the main road
until I had crossed the Allt Cruiniche by the bridge.
The climb to the top of the first ridge, about 1,000 feet
up, is arduous and mainly through long bracken.
The route then led across the top of the red scree
face which is a prominent feature of the lower slopes,
and towards the Allt Cruiniche. Here I encountered
the first of the many bogs which in a wet season lie
between this point and the top. One's first impulse
is to try to avoid the bogs, but this is hopeless, and it
is better just to walk right ahead, and get thoroughly
soaked at once. Nothing will keep the bog water
out—not even water-proofed boots ; but one soon
becomes accustomed to the squelch, which may be
alarming at first, but is soon forgotten. My feet
told the tale for many a day to come; the bog water
dyes them a deep nut-brown, and only time will
restore them to their natural colour.

I followed the course of the Allt Cruiniche until I
reached the confluence of two streams. Following

the tributary flowing from the western peak, I continued upwards, keeping well to the right of the stream. The western peak was now well within sight, but instead of appearing a beautiful sharp point as seen from Loch Etive, this angle of vision showed a long sloping ridge, with only a slight hump on its northern end. Undoubtedly the best views of Ben Cruachan are obtained from Loch Etive, just above the entrance to Glen Noe and from the rising ground at the foot of Deadh Choimhead on the old road to Oban.

The source of the stream, which rises at the foot of the ridge, was soon reached, and then I encountered the worst bog I had yet crossed ; but it was also the last, for once through it I found myself at the foot of the ridge where vegetation practically ceased. Above this point the mountain was a mass of broken granite : some boulders as large as an ordinary house, some wedged together, and some loose rubble.

It was here that I discovered the first landmark, a square boulder of huge dimensions with a flat top. It stands at an altitude of nearly three thousand feet. Each climber is supposed to throw up a stone, and it is now assuming the shape of a gigantic pyramid.

Until then I had only had some intermittent peeps of the surrounding country as I had been toiling up the bottom of a corrie ; but when the pyramid is rounded a view meets the eye which is stern, wild and impressive, a scene which a lover of Nature delights to see.

On the left and almost overhead rose the steep ridge which culminates in the western peak. In

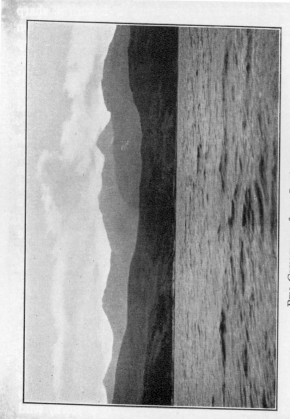

BEN CRUACHAN, from Loch Etive.

" . . . . . austere and awesome
Thou risest cloudward thy vows to render."

BEN CRUACHAN, Highest Peak, 3,689 feet.

front and across the valley rose Meall Cuanail, while northwards the beautifully symmetrical eastern peak of Cruachan, tapering into a perfect cone, reared its head to the height of 3689 feet. This is the highest point of the Cruachan range. There was a dread silence hanging over this amphitheatre of peaks, broken once by a distant crash, caused no doubt by a fall of rock down some precipitous slope into Glen Noe.

So far I had seen no wild life of any kind. I had not even heard the croak of the ptarmigan, or the call of the red grouse or the bark of the fox. All was silence—unbroken silence. On descending the mountain, however, by a different route I flushed quite a number of ptarmigan. Not one could I see until they rose, the colour of the birds harmonizes so well with their surroundings. A covey of not less than twelve were sitting on a lichen-covered rock, not two yards in front of me ; and although I was on the lookout I did not see them until they rose. The golden eagle is on the mountain, and I was keeping a sharp lookout for a pair that I had previously seen, and whose eyrie I had visited on Ben Trillichan near the top of Loch Etive, but they did not appear, nor did the peregrine falcons that I had expected to see.

The climb now became steeper and more toilsome as I picked my way amongst the great boulders which lie up the face of the western peak. Some fine views of the low-lying country are to be had on the way up. Dunstaffnage lay bathed in sunshine, with not a ripple on its silvery bay. A tiny white object like a needle rose out of the entrance to the Sound of Mull—the lighthouse on the green isle of Lismore—

E

while the crisp autumn air made the mountains of Mull and Morven stand out with keen sharpness. Just below and stretching northwards lay Loch Etive with its steep mountainous slopes, picturesquely scarred, down which rushed many streams. Lost here and there in deep gullies, but appearing again, a gleaming mass of white, they leapt downwards on their rugged course to the loch far below. What seemed to be a toy boat was just visible threading its way from pier to pier. It was the motor yacht *Loch Etive Queen* carrying His Majesty's mails from Ach-na-cloich to the top of the loch.

While gazing eastwards I saw great wisps of mist curling ominously around the eastern point, and as I was anxious to get on this peak, I decided to proceed no farther on the western ridge. Choosing what seemed to be the easiest way around the side of the spur I reached the ridge connecting the two peaks, which is about three thousand feet high. Once on the ridge the going was easier, but one had to be very careful, as at places it narrowed into quite a razor edge with a deep descent into Glen Noe. I heard a roaring sound, and noticed some distance ahead what seemed to be smoke pouring out of the rock. When I arrived at the spot I found that there was a dangerous funnel in the ridge reaching right down into Glen Noe, up which the mist from the glen was being blown, the noise caused by the wind being deafening. I shouted aloud but could not hear my own voice. Needless to say I did not waste much time there, a casual glance down this inferno being enough.

The two peaks are nearly a mile apart, and it had taken me an hour to cross the ridge and reach the top. The cone affords some fine rock scrambling, as it is very steep. Up there it was intensely cold, and the wind was so strong that I had to hold on. My hands soon became benumbed, and I was compelled to retreat about twenty yards, until I found a fissure in the rock large enough to hold me comfortably. Slipping off my rucksack I had the first real rest since I left Taynuilt in the early morning. It was delightful to lie there on that bright autumn day, and I wondered what it might be like a few weeks hence, for during the previous year, in the month of September, the snow lay deep on the mountain three-quarters of the way down. This is nothing remarkable among the high peaks, for I have been on Ben Lawers in the middle of August with the snow lying deep on the northern side, while on the southern side it was quite bare, and bathed in warm sunshine. That same day from the cairn I tried to pick up Ben Nevis, but it seemed to be smothered in what I took to be mist, but I learned two days later that at the time I was looking for it a blinding snowstorm was raging on the mountain.

Great masses of cumulus clouds, like snow drifts, had passed overhead at various times during the day, but while lying in my cosy nook I noticed a dense, black cloud creeping up the valley from the west, far below me. It was travelling at a considerable speed, and in a short time completely blotted out the whole landscape in front, which a few minutes before had been bright with sunshine. It was a curious effect to see the sun shining above, with all the peaks standing out clear and sharp as a cameo, while half-way down the hill side, and all around as far as I could see, was this dense black cloud. I photographed this strange phenomenon, and it turned out a very curious picture. Luckily the cloud passed away as quickly as it came, otherwise it would have spoilt the view of the extensive panorama which lay in front of me.

From its geographical position, as well as its height, some of the finest views in Scotland can be seen from the various peaks of Ben Cruachan. On a clear day you can trace the dim outline of the Outer Hebrides, with the sharp needle-like peaks of Rum standing out in bold relief, while the gnarled, fantastic shapes of the black Coolins appear to the north-east. In front many lochs and tarns come under notice, the most conspicuous being Loch Nell and Loch Feochan, while Loch Awe, like a narrow blue ribbon, stretches away almost to the horizon. If you cast your eye down Glen Aray you get a peep of the upper reaches of Loch Fyne, while far south, in the same line, Goat Fell, in Arran, appears dimly in the distance. Ben Lomond rears its head just beyond Ben Ime, while Ben Lui is a prominent feature in the east, and over its northern shoulder Ben More and Stobinian can be seen. In the far east Ben Lawers appears, while a point or two farther north and in the distance the pyramid of Schiehallion is just visible. Over the back, and due north, the huge bulk of Ben Nevis is clearly seen.

It is a stiff climb from the main road to the top, but once you have reached about two thousand feet the exertion is amply repaid by the marvellous view which gradually unfolds itself as you climb higher and higher.

THE SPIRIT OF LONE GLEN ETIVE.

"Where shadows deepen early and purple heather grows."

CHAPTER VII.

IN LONE GLEN ETIVE.

" Where shadows deepen early and purple heather grows."

HOW often have I been asked, where exactly is Glen Etive, and how do you get to it? It lies between the head of Loch Etive and the western fringe of Rannoch Moor at the Black Mount, and it is nearly fifteen miles long. Should you want to go there in the winter time, you would have a difficult problem to face, but things are quite different during the summer months. A well appointed motor boat runs daily from Ach-na-cloich pier, which stands in a beautifully sequestered bay about five miles east of Connel Ferry. The boat runs to the head of Loch Etive, carrying His Majesty's mails to a wide but very sparsely populated district containing one or two small grazing farms, shooting lodges and ghillies' houses. From there a very indifferent and rough road winds its way through the glen to King's House Inn, on the edge of the moor of Rannoch.

If the day is fine, and the mist and clouds have cleared from the mountains, the sail up the loch is delightful. Immediately after the boat leaves Ach-na-cloich the ruins of Ardchattan Priory are seen, founded in the thirteenth century by one of the Lords of Lorne. In this old ivy-covered priory King Robert the Bruce held a Parliament, said to be the last conducted in the Gaelic tongue. The beautifully wooded grounds at Airds Point, on the other side of the loch, are a pleasing feature in the landscape, and immediately opposite can be seen the entrance to Glen Salach, which runs through the hills to Barcaldine on Loch Creran.

The high cliffs of Ben Duirinnis appear on the left, while on the south can be seen the neat little village of Taynuilt, with its many outlying villas and old mansion houses nestling amongst the trees. The extensive granite quarries of Bonawe are on the opposite side, and just beyond this the loch narrows. After half an hour's sailing Glen Noe appears, a rugged valley running round the foot of Ben Cruachan and emerging on the main Oban road, a little beyond Kilchurn Castle on Loch Awe.

The loch now becomes less narrow (at its widest part it is about a mile and a half broad) and on looking back, one of the best views of Ben Cruachan is to be had. Here all the peaks of that wonderful mountain can be seen stretching in a long range, with the exception of Meall Cuanail, which lies behind the highest peak and just above the Pass of Awe.

Once more the loch narrows until you feel that you could almost put out your hand and touch the mountains, particularly when the mist lies on their slopes. It is extremely eerie in this part on a dull day, for you seem to be completely trapped on all sides. You are now abreast of Ben Starav with its peak often lost in the clouds, while on the other side Ben Trillichan rears its precipitous sides sheer out of the water; in a deep gash on its dark breast, on the top of an inaccessible cliff, is the home of the golden eagle.

Now you are completely surrounded by the high peaks, which rear their proud heads the one above the other, with the Shepherds of Etive towering above all in the background. On rounding a little headland a pier is seen close at hand. Here you land to begin the long tramp to the head of the glen.

At first the road is beautifully diversified with hazel and birch. A fine waterfall is passed beside a lonely shieling, and then the oak and the horse chestnut, intermingled with larch and rowan hanging heavy with scarlet berries, line the roadway as you near the post office. Beyond this the wooded country is left behind, and the road leads out into a wild mountainous track with peaks on either side, most of them covered with coarse grass with patches of rock protruding, some just bare rock and precipice, with the Etive flowing always in the valley below. Distant mountain torrents, only a white streak, are seen far up the slopes, but no sound can be heard, for they are too distant. Here and there a ghillie's hut stands in some lonely corner, but there is no sign of life, only the river and the everlasting hills.

For the first few miles the road rises and falls, but from Dalness, where it is three hundred feet up, there is a continual climb till it reaches King's House. A bridle path strikes north at Dalness and winds its way up the valley between the Little Shepherd and Bein Fhada, and after many a tortuous twist, and crossing various streams, it ultimately arrives in Glencoe, nearly opposite the cairn. This path, however, should only be taken by those who know it, as it is a little difficult to trace, and highly dangerous if the mist comes down. From Dalness the road and the river through Glen Etive run almost parallel until they reach a point nearly two miles from King's

House, where the road strikes north and joins the old highway through Glencoe.

There is really no wooded part or forest all the way, but just patches of pine at very distant intervals, and these always mark some lonely cot. Apparently they have been planted to protect the cottage from the gales that sweep with such force up the glen.

For miles that huge mountainous range consisting of many peaks, called Buachaille Etive Mor, completely dominates the glen on the west. To me it seems a peculiarly deceptive mountain, for you can see those peaks for miles before you really reach them. As the road winds and twists like a corkscrew they appear and reappear. Sometimes they seem close at hand, while at others they seem far distant. At some angles of vision their formation completely changes. There is one point, some time before Dalness appears in view, where two of the peaks look as if connected by a great suspension bridge, but from the next bend in the road, where the light penetrates from a different angle, you discover that this is an illusion.

This massive range culminates in the peak of Stob Dearg, 3,345 feet high. There it stands in its dread silence, immovable and impenetrable. This peak as seen from King's House looks like a gigantic sugar loaf rising out of the edge of the Moor of Rannoch, but the best view of it is to be had from the Glen Etive road a few miles before you reach Glencoe. From there you see it in all its rugged grandeur, primeval, twisted and torn asunder into enormous precipices, needle-like pinnacles and tortuous serrated peaks.

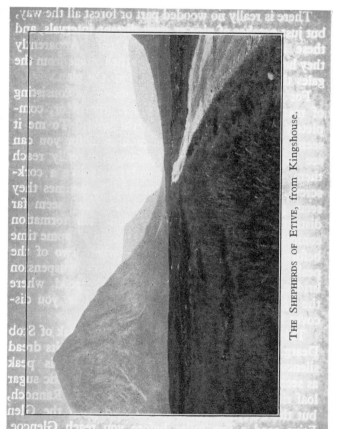

THE SHEPHERDS OF ETIVE, from Kingshouse.

"The road now seems to vanish in the mists and peat hags of the
lonely Moor of Rannoch."

Photo by Winifred Wilson.

KINGSHOUSE AND SRON-NA-CREISE.

"The scene of many stirring adventures when cattle reiving was in vogue."

" Peaks to the clouds that soar
  Corrie and fell where eagles dwell
  And cataracts dash evermore."

Surely when Nature made our Highland hills and
glens, Glencoe and Glen Etive must have been her
workshop ! With the exception of the Black Coolins
in Skye I know of nothing wilder than this.

It is a gloomy road to travel alone, and you will
have some idea of its loneliness when I tell you that,
with the exception of two ladies at Dalness shooting
lodge, I saw no one during my tramp from the head of
the loch to King's House, said to be thirteen to fifteen
miles. No one seems quite sure of the distance and
I saw no milestones to mark it.

Through all those solitary miles I had no other
company than the red deer on the mountain slopes,
and the meadow pipits, wagtails and whinchats in
the glen below, with here and there the piercing
call of a curlew, a sure sign that one is in close com-
munion with Nature in her sternest mood. A lordly
heron would sometimes rise from a stream and
survey me wth astonishment, then having satisfied
its curiosity with a few flaps of its stately wings it
would alight again some distance farther on. As I
passed through some swamps great pale blue dragon
flies were shimmering over them, while others were
darting to and fro over the pools like tiny gossamer-
winged fairies in a frolic. I did not see many wild
flowers of any note, but I had not much time to search
for them. Bog myrtle was, of course, everywhere
and its aromatic perfume was constantly wafted on the
breeze.

The road as far as Dalness is passable, but from there to the point where it joins the Glencoe road it fairly well resembles a dried-up river bed. Here and there are some fine waterfalls on tributaries that feed the Etive, but the best of all is on the Etive itself a little beyond Dalness. Here the roar of the river is deafening as it hurls itself over the rocks in a succession of leaps and bounds into a deep linn far below. The spray rises from the linn in showers and is wafted on the wind like spindrift by the seashore. A rope cradle-bridge is suspended across the gully near the head ghillie's house, and this frail structure has often to be used by the deer stalkers when the river is in flood.

Some distance beyond is the bleakest part of the glen. It becomes narrow and wild, with Bein Dearg on the one side and Sron-na-Creise on the other, but once you are through this pass, you see before you the open expanse of the Moor of Rannoch, and— welcome news—King's House Inn is in sight.

The rough surface of the road had made walking very heavy and I was carrying a weighty rucksack on my back, which was made heavier by the addition of some geological specimens picked up by the way. So when I arrived at the inn at about six o'clock I was both travel-stained and tired, and I rejoiced to see the kindly face of the hostess, who welcomed me in and was soon busy preparing a meal to which I did ample justice.

The inn is very old and must have been the scene of many stirring adventures when cattle reiving was in vogue and gentlemen of fortune passed that way. It is a rambling old building with narrow passages, and it may be of interest to anglers to learn that in a glass case on one of the mantelpieces in the long dining-room is a stuffed trout, weighing five and a half pounds, which was caught in one of the adjacent lochs. The inn must have stood the test of many a hurricane sweeping up the glen, and it is no wonder that the walls have been made three and a half feet thick, for it stands eight hundred feet above sea level, and I had ample proof of the fierceness with which the wind can sweep across the moor.

There is a tiny chamber underneath one of the rooms, entered by a trap door in the floor, where tradition says that Prince Charlie hid from his pursuers. I was not aware of the Prince having been so far south after Culloden, but, curiously enough, I was told that in Dalness Lodge one of their cherished possessions is a drinking cup, said to have been used by him.

King's House looks eastward into the wide expanse of desolate moor. The view would have been much finer had it looked westward, but the prevailing winds are from that direction, which would have made things lively in the front of the house.

The brown moorland, however, patched with heather of various hues of purple has a charm peculiarly its own, and the scene was made perfect the morning after my arrival by the appearance of an enormous herd of red deer which came over from Glen Etive. At first a pair of antlers appeared stealthily over a ridge, followed by another and another, until the whole herd was in sight. They scattered out and grazed peacefully as they moved along towards the inn. Suddenly the leading stag stopped, then tossed his antlers in the air, and stood gracefully at attention. The wind had changed, I suppose, and he smelt the taint of man on the breeze. He gave the herd some signal, for instantly they divided in two, one half crossing by the back of the inn and making northwards for the corries of Glencoe, while the others crossed in front with the sun shining gloriously on their red flanks as they bounded past. They were soon lost to sight in the wide and rolling waste which leads eastward to Loch Laidon.

The numberless bogs in the moor formed a happy hunting ground for the wild caterans in their ragged tartans in days gone by, and it was a simple matter for them to leap at the throat of the unwary traveller from behind one of the huge blocks of stone that lie scattered everywhere.

I stood on the old bridge close by the inn just as the shades of night were falling, and watched the fading colours of a beautiful sunset diffusing themselves through the mists that were gathering thick on Glencoe. As twilight fell a feeling of eeriness crept over me. I seemed to see crouching shadows creeping over the bridge, to vanish in the darkness that hung heavy on the inn. It made me think of the days of David Balfour and Alan Breck and John Splendid; so deeming discretion the better part of valour I knocked the ashes out of my pipe and retraced my steps to the front door. There I stood for a few minutes listening to the wail of some night bird which probably had lost its way in the depths of the moor. I then ascended the stair leading to my bedroom

The Vale of Weeping, from the Signal Rock.

" The Coe, the limpid Cona of Ossian."

and turned in for the night, not, as was the custom in days of yore, with a dirk and pistol lying on my pillow, but with the wind sighing and moaning in the gnarled old fir trees that swayed to and fro in the blast.

CHAPTER VIII.

GLOOMY GLENCOE.

" The wind comes down with a moan and a sigh
And a voice, like the voice of a wail and a cry,
The lonely traveller hears."

Blackie.

WHAT a legion of memories crowd upon us
at the mention of " The Vale of Weeping."
If we were only gifted with the second sight, as many
of the natives are said to be, and could penetrate
through the strange, uncanny mists that gather up at
King's House, and come creeping down the lonesome
glen towards the fall of a winter's night, we might
get a peep into that dim and distant past when men
sometimes found it safer to be amongst the heather
than under the shelter of a thatched roof. Probably,
however, it is better that we should not !

No name in history is more fraught with painful
memories than that of gloomy Glencoe. But why
gloomy ? True, you can see it when the morning
breaks grey and leaden, and drizzling rain and mist
hang around the many peaks that hem it in, and
threaten a dismal day. You may then call it gloomy
if you like, but to the true lover of the mountains that
is just the kind of morning on which to see the glen.
And should the drizzle cease, and the mist begin to
rise, great wisps swirling and twisting like writhing
serpents round the high peaks, while it creeps from
the valley below up the scaurs like smoke clouds and
spreads itself across the mountains, then you will be

glad that you came to the glen that day. Look across the valley and you will see masses of mist slumbering in the corries that encircle " The Three Sisters," and then creep upwards to gather like an aureole round their heads, bringing forcibly before you their other name, " Faith, Hope and Charity." The sun breaks through, and its silvery shafts pierce the mist like searchlights : then, indeed, you see Glencoe at its best.

The valley is composed of two glens—the one wooded, shady, fertile and green, while the other consists of great bleak, volcanic peaks towering up into the sky and looking down with proud disdain on all puny things below.

Perhaps the best way to see the glen is to enter it over that well known landmark, the old Bridge of Coe. But let us first take the little path which leads past some neat thatched cottages to the mound on which is erected a beautiful Celtic cross to com-memorate the massacre which took place in the early morning of 13th February, 1692. The view from this point is both impressive and commanding. Slumber-ing at your feet on a peaceful summer day is the little sleepy hollow with its occupants busy at their hay, while a filmy mist like incense pervades all around. Several cottages are dotted here and there, while smoke, curling up amongst the trees, shows where others are hidden. In front, the tall symmetrical cone of Meall Mor stands boldly out of the shimmer-ing haze, and is flanked by the long flung ridges and humps of Bidean-nam-Bian, the highest mountain in Argyllshire. From our coign of vantage the whole countryside seems beautifully wooded, but the visitor for the first time has yet to learn of another glen, the real Glencoe, which lies beyond the old inn of Clachaig.

No wonder that the people love their old home-steads ! They are born and brought up in the atmos-phere of the glen, an atmosphere which the man in the street does not understand. He wonders how any one could exist in such a stark and lonely place, but he has never felt the call of the wild in his blood, for the city does not produce such a thing ; he does not understand what the glens or the mountains or the isles mean to those who know and love them.

It chanced one day that an old man and I foregathered in the glen, a man well over the three score years and ten, but still alert, keen and active. I shall never forget the ring that was in his voice and the light that gleamed in his eye as he told me an unwritten tale of the massacre handed down for generations in his family. His life story is the tale of many others. He had left the glen when a youth to seek his fortune in Canada. He had had his ups and downs, but was always buoyed up with the thought that some day, however late it might be, he would be able to come back to spend the remainder of his life in the peace and quiet of his own Glencoe. He was a Macdonald, and proud of his name, and with a triumphant look on his face he said, " I was born in the glen, and here I am come back to die there."

This is only one example of many that one comes across while wandering in the glens and the isles of Scotland. It is always the same story. It matters not how many years it may be—" The blood is strong, the heart is Highland." The old desire to return

GLEN COE, from the "Study."

"Westward down the glen the view is grand. The road twists
into the distance like an enormous snake."

FALLS OF CONA, GLENCOE.

" *The clear crystal Cona is ever rushing onwards.*"

burns fiercely like a beacon, and a voice still calls them back—back—back.

Now let us retrace our steps to the bridge which carries the traffic over the Coe, the limpid Cona of Ossian. It has become the habitat of the little fern *asplenium trichomanes* (black spleenwort). Here it flourishes to perfection and adds a charm to the old world structure. There are two deep pools on either side of the bridge, and the Cona is such a beautifully clear river that one's eye could easily see to their shingly bottom. When leaning on the bridge one hot autumn day I noticed several large objects moving lazily about in the pool below. I watched them very intently for some time. They were salmon, but they were evidently out for a lazy day, for while at times they would rise to the surface, they soon sank to the bottom again. Who could blame them, for it was too hot for anything that day! But while the king of fish might laze about at his will I had to shoulder my rucksack and trudge up the glen, for the day was well advanced and there still lay twelve long Highland miles before me.

The glen is extremely beautiful at this point; the road twists and twines through an avenue of beech, ash, pine, scrub oak and hazel. You could almost imagine you were in the Trossachs were it not for the river which appears every here and there. Fine glimpses are to be had through the trees of the many rugged peaks which form the glen, the principal one at this point being Meall Mor. A high rock can be seen on the right hand side a little before reaching Clachaig Inn—(they call it Clachaig Hotel now, but surely the old name of inn is better suited to the

F

locality !) This rock is named the " Signal Rock," for tradition says that it was there that the signal was given for the commencement of the massacre.

As viewed from the road the rock does not seem to command a very imposing position for such a purpose, but in reality it rises to a height of 130 feet, and the view from the top is very extensive, as it overlooks both sides of the glen as far as the old bridge of Coe. Down the centre of the landscape flows the Cona in a long series of zigzags till it is lost to sight at the bridge. Towards the north, thick woods fringe the steep slopes of Sgor-nam-Fiannaidh and the Pap of Glencoe, while on the south the rugged peak of Meall Mor frowns down upon you through the faint blue haze which haunts its many corries, suggesting some hidden mystery there.

The rock rises from a dense wood of spruce fir which almost surrounds an ornamental serpentine lake well stocked with trout. The little path to the top passes through a dense undergrowth of bracken and other ferns and creepers of many hues. When the top is reached you find yourself in the centre of a fairyland of beauty ; in fact, this is one of the beauty spots of Scotland, though few visitors ever see it. This part of the glen is private property and the many people who pass along the highway are all unconscious of the beautiful scenery so near at hand, only obscured by a narrow ridge running behind another little lake close to the highway.

A scramble through the woods discloses every here and there heaps of stones, which probably at one time were homesteads, and tell their own tale. A deep ravine circling the woods reveals the course of the Cona which can be seen far below rushing along its rocky shelving bed. The ravine is spanned at one part by a light iron bridge, and following an almost obliterated track through the heather and bog you arrive at Achnacan, where it is said that the old chief, MacIan, and his sons lived at the time of the massacre. Doubtless the country all around would be practically devoid of trees then, and, if that were so, a fire kindled on the flat top of the rock would easily be seen for miles around, so that there is every reason to believe that this little eminence is rightly named the " Signal Rock," and that it played a very important part on that tragic morning when snow fell heavily on hill and dale.

While lying on the rock and steeping oneself in the atmosphere of the glen one conjures up strange and stirring scenes that may have happened all around, scenes in which the ragged tartan and the dirk played a leading part ; but probably it is better to ring down the curtain on that period and forget about a time when clan feuds were unceasing and life was held too cheaply.

On leaving the " Signal Rock," you are immediately confronted with Aonach Dubh, a huge mass of porphyritic rock rising sheer from the roadside. The road here twists round its northern end, and the lonely Tarn of Achtriochtan appears in view. High above the lochan is to be seen Ossian's shower bath, where a cataract breaks on the face of a cliff. A little farther along, Ossian's cave appears high up in the face of the rock.

Just beyond, you cross the dried-up bed of a stream

which in winter comes down the corries of Meall Dearg, whose two jagged teeth stand boldly out defying the elements. This stream, just before it reaches the Cona, must be at least fifty yards wide, and its bed is a mass of enormous boulders and stones washed down from above. The road at some parts here is just like a river bed too. In fact, despite the efforts of the roadmen, a great many parts of it all the way up the glen are much the same.

There is no vegetation of any account amongst the mountains, just coarse grass and bracken patched in here and there amongst the frowning, weeping peaks. Trees there are none, with the exception of a few sturdy Scotch pines on the borders of the lochan of Achtriochtan, which sway and sigh in the blast like the lost spirits that haunt the narrow glen.

A ghillie's cottage is reached a few miles farther on, and just opposite the cottage on the other side can be seen a deep ravine leading straight up the mountain side to a large amphitheatre between two ridges. It was up this gully that the cattle were driven after a foray of the MacDonalds on some adjoining clan, and once there they were perfectly safe. One wonders how cattle could climb up such a place, but the wild caterans of that day saw to that, and their motto doubtless was " needs must when the devil drives."

You are now under the shadow of " The Three Sisters," but there is still a steep and arduous climb before you reach the cairn. There is a beautiful waterfall just opposite the cairn, but it is in a dangerous place, and one slip on the sloping rocks would mean a sheer fall into the Cona, which can be seen plunging and rushing along in showers of spray at the bottom of the ravine.

One of the best views of the glen can be had from the cairn. On the south " The Three Sisters " seem to dominate everything. They are quaint creatures, and are seen at their best with the mist hanging around their venerable brows. Away up on their topmost peaks they are scarred and riven beyond all hope—but they must be seen and not described.

Westward down the glen the view is grand. The road twists into the distance like an enormous snake. It has a fall of eight hundred feet in four miles; sometimes the gradient is very steep and sometimes gradual. Here the road zigzags round hairpin bends until it is lost to view behind an outlying spur of " The Study," and there it is again clinging and creeping round the giddy precipices of " The Chancellor." Far down in the glen the clear crystal Cona is ever rushing onwards till it mingles with the waters that guard the sacred isle of St. Munda.

A new road is at present under construction through Glencoe, which, when completed, will doubtless delight the hearts of motorists. What its effect may be in changing the general aspect of one of our grandest and wildest glens remains to be seen. The new road from " The Study " down to Clachaig Inn, will run at a lower elevation than the present one, and it is somewhere about " The Study " that the greatest change will take place. It is to be hoped that the wild nature of the glen will not be destroyed at this point. The new road, however, will be a pleasure in disguise to the wanderers with the rucksack, for they will be left to tramp the old road unmolested, while their less fortunate brethren will be rushing through below at top speed to Ballachulish Ferry.

About a mile beyond the cairn, and just opposite the peak of Stobnan Cabar, the road reaches its highest point, 1,011 feet, while a mile farther on is the " Devil's staircase," a precipitous track, crossing the mountains to the head of Loch Leven. From this point onwards the road winds its weary way through bog and heather with the Great and Little Shepherds towering above. A dim silhouette of King's House Inn now appears in the far distance, and the road then seems to vanish in the mists and peat hags of the lonely Moor of Rannoch.

CHAPTER IX.

AMONGST THE CLOUDS.

" Where essential silence cheers and blesses
  And forever in the hill recesses
  Her more lovely music broods and dies."
  Stevenson.

I WAS once living near the foot of one of the highest
mountains in Scotland, and for six weeks the
top had never been seen owing to dense masses of
cloud hanging over it. I wanted to get up into that
cloud, to see what it looked like, and so I started off
early one morning.

As I tramped along the riverside I found the glen
teeming with wild life of all kinds. Great gaily-
painted dragon flies were flitting about the banks of
the stream, hesitating and darting hither and thither
in a manner peculiar to their kind. Small birds with
gay plumage flew from bush to bush, apparently
objecting to my intrusion in their domain. A pair
of rather curious birds passed overhead, flying so
low that I had no difficulty in recognizing them as
cormorants, evidently making for the sea loch close
at hand. Busily feeding on a mud flat were quite
a number of sandpipers, with their dull brown
plumage, pretty mottled breasts, and long legs.
Oyster-catchers were also numerous. I can never
understand why they are so called ; I do not think
they live on oysters, though they devour greedily
enough shell fish cast up on the sea shore. Their

plumage is black and white, and they have long pink legs and vermilion beaks.   Dippers were also numerous, flying in their quaint way from rock to rock, flicking up their little stumpy tails every time they rose.

Shortly after leaving them behind I reached the foot of the mountain, and began my upward climb of five miles to the summit.   It was a beautiful morning, and the sun was shining brightly.   I passed a shelter hut considerately placed for tired climbers, or for refuge in case of storms, and some beautiful waterfalls, which seemed to come pouring out of the sky, as I could see nothing but clouds above them. I rested at the shelter hut and took some photographs, and surveyed all the valley below me bathed in hot sunshine.   Great bluff peaks were standing up all around, riven and rent asunder at some early age. A little lochan nestled in a hollow of the mountain almost at my feet, while stretching in front for miles was a long, narrow sea loch.   Between two great peaks on my left could be seen a rugged gorge with a beautiful waterfall at its upper end.   So alluring did this corrie appear that I explored it a few days later.

I could not see what was above me for projecting rocks, but after I had climbed above them and reached a height of probably three thousand feet I was conscious of thin little films of mist swirling towards me. The higher I climbed the thicker became the mist until I found that I was almost enveloped in it. Everything around had disappeared as if by magic, dense thick vapour floated past me, and a deathly silence reigned.   Now and then the hoarse croak of the white grouse or the mew of the buzzard could be heard coming from some corrie near at hand, but with that exception all sound was shut out, and I was alone in the clouds. The higher I climbed the thicker became the dull grey vapour until I could only see a yard or so in front of me, and even the rocks seemed to be of the same dull grey colour. I looked longingly for some vista of blue sky ahead, but in vain. I was buried in the cloud. I still had hopes of getting above it, but, alas, after some more hard climbing I reached the top, over 4,000 feet up, only to find it seemed to be getting darker up there. I stumbled about in this dim solitude for some time, and while doing so discovered for the first time that I was thoroughly drenched. Again I looked in vain for blue sky, and at last decided that it would be useless to remain any longer, so started on my downward journey. I had to take my bearings very carefully, for there were no landmarks to be seen. I had also to pick my way cautiously in case of a slip, and after scrambling downwards for a long time, always keeping in a westerly direction, I began to think that the clouds must reach right down into the valley now and that it must be raining heavily there.

At last I began to see farther ahead, and tall rocks about ten or twenty yards away loomed up like ghosts. The cloud was becoming more of a thin mist and was sweeping along the mountain side like smoke. What was that ahead ? Something resembling a searchlight flashed through the mist, and suddenly I walked out into brilliant sunshine, to discover that there had been no rain at all down in the valley.

My attempt to get above the clouds that day had

been a failure. But the following morning as I rose early I was charmed to see the beautiful spectacle of the whole mountain enveloped in clouds, with the peaks standing out clear above them. As I gazed I was again seized with the burning desire to try to get above the clouds, and I thought if they remained as they were then, there was a possibility, so I set off.

It was a beautiful morning; the air was sharp and cold with just a slight touch of frost in it. The dew was hanging thick on the hedgerows, for the sun, although beginning to gain strength, was not yet strong enough to dry it up. I reached the place where I intended to leave the road, and leaping the old dry stone dyke, disturbed a flock of sheep that were lying quietly behind it. Crossing a little patch of bog and heather, and wading through a wilderness of brown bracken I began to climb with great eagerness, for the big cloud was still hanging above me. The ascent was very steep for the first thousand feet, and when I reached that height and halted to gain my breath, I discovered that this cloud was going to be another elusive pimpernel, for there it was, still high above me, and apparently rising more quickly than I could climb. It was going to be a race for the top with long odds in favour of the cloud. On I struggled for an hour, over rocks, up the banks of streams, through corries, but getting no nearer to the cloud. Arrived on a plateau from which the first peak rose, I saw that it was hopeless, as the cloud had almost passed off. All the peaks were nearly clear, and so I gave up the chase, and resolved to content myself by spending the day with wild nature.

I climbed the highest peak. The air was perfectly

still and breathless, with a warm sun shining, so I lay down amongst the rocks to rest and survey the beautiful panorama stretched around me. From that height I could see nearly all the islands comprising the Outer and Inner Hebrides, and the sea was like a sheet of burnished silver, stretching away out into the dim Atlantic. As I gazed out across the broad expanse of water, it became less bright, and ultimately assumed a leaden hue. This I noticed was caused by a dense black cloud rolling in towards the coast. Very soon the islands were gone, so was the sea. As the cloud reached the mainland it spread out in a fan-like shape, and all in its wake was lost to sight. It was a nimbus cloud of immense size, and was travelling towards me at great speed. I looked around, but there was no shelter anywhere, and so I patiently awaited results. I expected forked lightning to flash forth at any moment, and lightning on the mountains is very dangerous. None came, however, but in a very few minutes, hill, dale, loch and moor, all around me, were completely lost to sight—nothing but the high peaks stood out above that seething mass which rolled along a few hundred feet below. To my delight I saw that I was in a different air stratum from the cloud, for while it was bright and warm and still all around me, the air current beneath was travelling at great speed. There I sat on my high peak like the genie of the mountains, looking down on that strange phenomenon, a sea of rolling ink. It heaved, and twisted and piled itself up, mass above mass of ugly black moisture like dense smoke, and I knew it must be raining in torrents down below.

I had often looked at a rain cloud above and been curious to know what it would be like up there, but it was the first time that I had ever sat and looked down upon the upper surface of one, and from what I saw of it I thanked my lucky star that I was not in it.

CHAPTER X.

SHETLAND—THE ULTIMA THULE OF THE ROMANS.

> " And ever under and behind all song, the voice of
> the great sea, full of undefinable mystery, as of a
> half-remembered dream."—*Robertson*.

THE Shetland islands, about a hundred in number,
and forming the most northerly county in
Scotland, are bounded on the west by the Atlantic
Ocean, and on the east by the North Sea, and by their
peculiar situation may be said to form a boundary
line between those two frolicsome waters. The
islands are of the most irregular formation. The
largest is the Mainland, a little over fifty-five miles
in length, and about twenty-five miles at its widest
part, but the coast is so indented that to walk round
it would mean a tramp of nearly five hundred miles.
A glance at the map will show that it looks like a
lizard sprawling lazily on the surface of the water,
and making futile attempts to swallow up the northern
islands of Yell, Unst and Fetlar. The remainder of
the group, with a few exceptions, are very small—
some of them very picturesque, others very fantastic
in shape, and some so small and perpendicular that
they scarcely afford sufficient footing even for the
sea birds.

The Mainland is so extremely irregular in form that
it is a wonder a map of it can be drawn at all, at least
with any degree of accuracy, and the Ordnance Sur-

vey sheet speaks volumes for the patience and the intelligence of the surveyors. It is so intersected with voes (arms of the sea) that it is said that nowhere are you more than three miles from salt water. At many points the road runs for miles along a narrow neck of land, with the playful Atlantic on the one side, and the sullen North Sea on the other, little more than a hundred yards separating the two. On a stormy day the waves lash the rocks on either side with a fury that throws the spray high into the air.

The interior of the Mainland is of an undulating character, with every here and there sharp hills. None of the hills rises to any great height, with the exception of Ronas Hill, which rises above the voe of that name, and is 1475 feet high. Apart from small portions of grazing land towards the shore the interior consists mainly of peat bog and stunted heather, and there are a great number of fresh water lochs where excellent fishing can be had. None of these lochs is of any great size, but they afford capital sport, and some beautiful trout have been taken out of them.

The scenery is entirely different from what we are accustomed to see in most parts of Scotland, there being a great lack of trees on the islands. No tree will grow above the shelter of a protecting wall. There is a garden in Scalloway where a considerable number of ornamental trees were once planted, but not one would grow except where protected from the gale, and it seemed as if they had been carefully cut across whenever they reached the height of the wall.

The climate, considering that the islands lie so far north, is mild on the whole, no doubt due to the influence of the Gulf Stream. The atmosphere during the winter months is rather moist. The inhabitants, however, seem very healthy considering the severe climatic conditions to which they are subjected.

Ronas Hill, like most of the other hills and cliffs in North Mavine, is composed of red granite, though it is very unlike them in shape. Ronas is rounded, and comparatively smooth, while they are like the Shetland ponies that haunt their slopes—as wild and rugged as can well be imagined. The view from the top of the hill is very extensive and charming. Let us climb to the top, and look around. Over fourteen hundred feet below, like a broad silver ribbon glittering in the noonday sun, and studded here and there with the brown sails of the fishing boats, lies Ronas Voe—a long arm of the sea stretching for miles inland. In front, almost as far as the eye can reach, is a sepia coloured landscape of stunted heather, intersected every here and there with great black patches ; these are peat bogs, and the tiny black dots, running in long regular lines, are the stacks of peats drying for the winter fuel. What is that strange little thing like a snake, twisting and wriggling through the moors and bogs, and always appearing again, until it seems to melt into space ? It is the road from Hillswick to Lerwick, distant some forty miles—a weary road when you have to walk it, and conveyances are scarce in Shetland. Away to the west stretches the magnificent Bay of St. Magnus—one of the grandest bays in the world. I have climbed the Apennines on a perfect Italian summer day to view the famous Bay of Genoa, fringed with olive and orange groves, and for rugged grandeur it must yield the palm to St. Magnus Bay. The Heads of Grocken stand out in bold relief in the foreground, and many of the glorious sunsets, for which Shetland is famous, are to be seen there. As the sun begins to sink, the rest of the promontory is delicately flushed, then reflected light from the great ruddy ball catches the veins of porphyry that intersect the cliffs and plays up and down its scarred face like liquid fire. The sun sinks lower and lower till the Heads of Grocken stand out inky black in a sea of shimmering gold. Great streamers of deep orange and red shoot upwards and the sky gleams as if on fire long after the sun has disappeared.

Some of the finest cliff scenery in Great Britain stretches along the coast as far as Papa-Stour, while the Drongs and the Door Holm, pierced by an enormous arch, are conspicuous rocks in the bay. Some of the cliffs are truly awe-inspiring. They rear their serrated heads to the height of a thousand feet, and look defiantly down like mighty giants upon the angry waves below.

If you cast your eye in a direct line over Papa-Stour, you will notice a tiny black dot on the horizon, apparently floating on the bosom of the waters. It is the lonely island of Foula, which lies sixteen miles south-west of the nearest point of the Mainland, and is probably the most distinctive of the whole group. It has been asserted by some historians that Foula was the Ultima Thule of the Romans, and must have been the island that Agricola saw (according to Tacitus, his biographer) from the northern shores of Orkney, while others hold that it must have been all

HILLSWICK, SHETLAND.

Rona's Voe and Hill, Shetland.

the islands composing the group.   It is said, however, that the old Norse language, legends and customs lingered longer on Foula than in any other part of Shetland.   It is about three miles long, and two broad, and is used as a fishing station.   The eastern portion of the island is level, but on the west side the cliffs range from a thousand to twelve hundred feet high. There are five conical peaks on this side, and the highest, called the Sneug, is 1,372 feet.   For a long time Foula was famous for feathers and eggs, and its inhabitants boasted of their skill as cragsmen.   So fearless did they become that they seemed to look upon death on the crags as their ultimate end, for it became a saying on Foula, " My gutcher (grand-father) gaed afore, my faither gaed afore, and ower da Sneug I'll ging too."   The great skua gull still breeds on the island.   It is the largest and fiercest of its kind. Its body measures about twenty-five inches long, and its wings from tip to tip about forty-two inches.   It is a terror to all the feathered race—even the eagle gives it a wide berth.   As a fighter it is seen at its best defending its eggs or young, and during that period will defiantly attack a man.   It swoops from the air with terrific force and strikes him on the head with its feet as it rushes past.   The skua is dark brown in colour, and builds its nest, not on the crags like other gulls, but on the heather or grass.

Let us now turn our eyes to the east coast.   There chaos baffles description, for all Shetland can be seen in one panoramic stretch from Unst to Sumburgh Head, and on a clear day as far as the Fair Isle.   Lochs, voes, sea and islands are heaped together in endless confusion; while the eye tries to piece together the

G

whole into one picture, the brain seems to whirl and get confused. It is no use trying to give a further pen-picture of this endless land-and-seascape : it has to be seen to be admired.

The only towns on the Mainland are Lerwick and Scalloway, both of considerable size, and well supplied with first class hotels. Lerwick is the capital, and has an imposing appearance as you enter the harbour. The old town consists of a number of narrow streets and alleys, but the new town has some wide streets and handsome buildings, including the town hall. There are some excellent shops in both towns, but these have to supply the whole of the islands, and it is not to be wondered at that provisions in some of the outlying parts are sometimes scarce, particularly in stormy weather. At rare intervals in the outlying districts a small store is to be found, but you may have to tramp ten or fifteen miles to find it. Shops in Shetland are like oases in the desert—few and far between.

The chief industry, of course, is fishing, as there is very little land to be cultivated. Most of the natives, however, in the country districts are both crofters and fishermen. They have little crofts, situated often in groups in the immediate vicinity of a voe. The dwelling house consists generally of a but and a ben. The walls are made of rough unhewn stones, cemented together with clay and sand, and the roof is covered with layers of thin turf supported on rafters, and thatched with straw or reeds. In many cases the roofing is done in a primitive fashion, with the result that during the storms in winter the water often percolates and the buildings become very damp.

The floor consists of a mixture of earth and clay—a hole or two here and there being disregarded. The walls are generally hung round with fishing nets, and a few rough chairs complete the furnishings. There are always a few dogs lying about, and the pigs and the pet lambs are constant visitors. Cows are not numerous on these crofts, there being little or no grazing for them, but they generally have a good many sheep. Not only do the sheep keep up the food supply, but their wool is in constant demand for the knitting industry.

The Shetland crofters, unlike those in the western islands, are in fairly easy circumstances. The men go to the " haaf " or deep sea fishing from May to July, and can generally make as much from this as will pay the rent and supply the necessaries of life. Then the herring fishing lasts from July to September, and from the proceeds of this they can clothe themselves and their families. The women are experts at the knitting of shawls, and in many of the houses are to be found an excellent selection of these goods at the most moderate prices. The elder women with failing eyesight generally knit the coarser shawls, and stockings, while the girls produce work of the delicacy of a spider's web. It takes a girl weeks to knit one of these soft fleecy-looking garments, and you may take it for granted that she is not overpaid for her work. Of course by the time the shawl passes through the hands of the middleman and reaches Edinburgh, Glasgow or London it is priced at a very different figure from that which the maker receives.

I found the natives of these remote northern islands an honest, unsophisticated class of people. They made no attempt at the common practice of trying to take you in. Nowhere, in all my wanderings, did I find that I was overcharged for anything, but in many cases I felt that they were too modest in their demands. I left the islands feeling happy that here at least was a race of people, quite contented with their surroundings, who had not yet learned to worship at the shrine of the golden calf.

HERRING CLEANING, HILLSWICK.

" Wha'll buy my caller herrin' ? "

CHAPTER XI.

YACHTING AMONGST THE WESTERN ISLES.

"The blue islands are pullin' me away,
Their laughter puts the leap upon the lame."
Macleod.

I MADE a cruise some time ago with a medical friend amongst the western islands. He was interested in botany, and I in ornithology, and my chief object was to see something of wild bird life out there. Our ultimate goal was St. Kilda, where I had made many good friends on previous visits.

Our route lay through some of the wildest and most rugged of our island scenery, a land steeped in history and romance, which has inspired the pen of both poet and historian. The artist has found ample scope for his brush in the marvellous sunsets among the isles, and in the ever-changing lights and shades on the water. With the exception, perhaps, of the sunsets I saw on the Heads of Grocken in Shetland, nowhere else do I remember having seen such splashes of crimson and gold and delicate saffron. As the sun slowly dips into the water, all around becomes a picture of vivid crimson.

We left the Clyde one summer evening on our long trek over the waterway to the isles. As we passed Arran the dim outline of Goatfell was just visible against the sky. The moon rose as we sailed past Holy Isle, and we had the delightful prospect before us of rounding the Mull of Kintyre under a full moon.

Next morning found us running up the Sound of Islay. Away on our starboard side the rugged Paps of Jura were standing out clear in the cold grey sky, while the whole island presented a landscape of bleak moor and bog.

In delightful contrast the green pasture lands of Islay stretched away on the port side. We had little time to spare there, and only ran into Port Askaig for an hour or two. Shortly after leaving Port Askaig we passed the two famous Islay distilleries, and on emerging into the open sea our course was laid for the historic little Island of Colonsay, which is joined to Oronsay at low water by a long stretch of sand. There is no pier at Scalasaig Bay, and passengers are transferred to and from the beach and the steamer by means of a luggage boat. There is a good hotel and plenty of sea and loch fishing. The monument on the top of the hill overlooking the bay was erected to a former owner of the island. There are some fine ruins of a priory on Oronsay, and many old sculptured stones are scattered about. The Oronsay Cross is well known as one of the finest specimens of old Celtic work.

On leaving Colonsay we steered a north-west course for Tiree. Shortly after rounding the point, we had a fine view of the twin peaks of Ben Cruachan and the mountains of Mull, while the Torran rocks lay just ahead. It was on these rocks that the Brig "Covenant" foundered in Stevenson's story, *Kidnapped*, although for the purpose of the story the author located them farther to the north. Shortly after passing the Torrans we had a distant view of the sacred isle of Iona with the Treshnish Isles lying farther north, the one calling for most notice being the fantastic Dutchman's Cap.

We reached Scarnish in Tiree a little before dusk. Both Coll and Tiree are low, flat, sandy islands, and one wonders why the Atlantic when in a surly mood does not wash them away. So flat is Tiree that we actually saw the houses long before we saw the island, and one gets the impression that they are standing in the water. There was no pier at Scarnish then, just a slip where a small boat could land. It is very exposed and often stormy, and the landing of passengers there was at times exceedingly dangerous and carried out to their great discomfort. During the winter months it was nothing unusual for weeks to elapse before steamers could land provisions. Large heavy rowing boats were used for this purpose, and horses, cattle and sheep were all transferred in this way.

I was early awake the following morning, for I wished to get some photographs of the island of Rum. I feared from previous experiences that we were not likely to be allowed to land, and this was so. We had to content ourselves with sailing round the forbidden island, with the great peaks of Oreval, Halival, Haskeval and Scour-na-Gillian rising sheer out of of the water, and towering in their majesty above us. The island seems to be intersected by two great glens, where the old red deer roam undisturbed. It is one of the most rugged of the smaller islands of the Inner Hebrides.

It was still early when we came within sight of the misty isle of Skye. It is a wonderful moment when you see it for the first time. There is something weird and uncanny in those great black, rugged peaks, torn and rent asunder in ages long since past, and as you slowly creep up Loch Scavaig under their shadow, you are conscious of being in one of the most lifeless and desolate places in Scotland. I have never been lucky enough to see the sun set there, but on a previous visit I saw it rise on wild Loch Scavaig, and never will I forget it. I have seen a sunrise painting the Mediterranean with delicate tints and shades, but it was tame compared with the weird magnificence of what I saw on those scarred and misty peaks.

We landed in Loch Scavaig, and after a scramble over rough boulders and jagged rocks for less than a quarter of a mile the little gem of the Coolins—Loch Coruisk—burst into view. "Coruisk" means the water cauldron. When seen with the sun shining on its unruffled surface, it sparkles and scintillates like a diamond, but when the sky threatens, and a dense pall hangs over Sgurr Alasdair, it becomes a witches' cauldron of inky blackness. Nothing seems to live there—but what could live with the perpetual gloom of these vast hills cast over it? Some of the higher peaks are seldom entirely visible, and great masses of black vapour and cold grey mist roll up and down their scarred and riven sides. At times when the sun penetrates this pall, the sharp, saw-like peaks can be seen standing out in bold relief, but it is only for a minute. From morn till night there is the ceaseless sighing and moaning of the wind as it rushes up and down the corries, while here and there, as the death-like curtain rises and falls, some rushing torrent can be seen dashing itself into spray amongst

The Gem of the Black Coolins—
LOCH CORUISK, SKYE.

"Where the sun's kindly radiance seldom gleams;
Where some tall peak, defiant, steadfast, mocks
The passing gods."

Photo by Winifred Wilson.

RUINS OF KISIMUL CASTLE, CASTLE BAY.

the boulders below.   Such is the scene in which Loch Coruisk is laid.

The scenery all along the west coast of Skye is very rugged.   On nearing Talisker Bay the famous distillery of that name can be seen standing between two high hills.   Loch Harport is reached immediately after passing Talisker, and at the top of the loch is Carbost Pier, from which the main road leads through Glen Drynoch to Sligachan Inn, the great Skye centre for climbers.   In Glen Drynoch you are brought face to face with the crofter question, for there you find huts in which it is almost impossible to think that people live.

As we crossed Loch Bracedale, and passed Idrigill Point we saw Macleod's Maidens ahead.   These are a group of three rocks rising to a considerable height, and bearing a wonderful resemblance to female figures.

Loch Dunvegan is very picturesque towards the head.   Dunvegan Castle is one of the oldest inhabited castles in Scotland.   It contains a collection of Jacobite relics, including a flowered silk vest and a drinking cup which belonged to Prince Charlie, and a portion of the famous lock which Lady Macdonald informs us Flora " clipit wi' her ain hands frae his lang yellow hair."

The castle has a magnificent situation, being built on a rock which is now joined to the mainland by a bridge.   Originally the only access to the castle was from the sea by a narrow flight of steps cut in the rock leading to the main door.   When approached by the present roadway it has a massive solid appearance but loses much of its ancient grandeur.   The finest view is from the slopes of the shore where the old grey turrets, standing out against a background of dark green foliage, make a perfect picture of hoary antiquity. The " keep " is the oldest part of the castle; it is said to have been built in the tenth century, but some historians ascribe it to the twelfth or thirteenth. The walls of the drawing room, which was the ancient hall at one time, are nine feet thick. A trap door in the floor of a dark room near the hall leads to the dungeon, which is cut out of the solid rock on which the castle stands. The fairy tower was built in the sixteenth century and contains a room at the top which is said to be haunted. The castle has been modernized in many respects, but the narrow staircase to the top of the tower still remains as it was originally built. Sir Walter Scott and Dr. Johnson slept in this room during their respective visits, and one wonders how the doctor got his ponderous body up such a narrow stair; unfortunately, Boswell has not chronicled what he said when he reached the top. Dunvegan Castle has been the scene of many dark deeds, and if its old walls could speak they would tell some queer tales.

We crossed the Minch and came in time to Castle Bay in brilliant sunshine. The first thing that strikes a stranger is the ruin of Kisimul Castle, standing out in bold relief on a rock in the bay. The little town is quite charming with its many pretty cottages dotted along the face of the rocks. During the fishing season it is quite a sight to see the boats putting out to sea.

On a previous visit I had found the Barra crofters, like some of their neighbours in Skye, living in tumble-down huts, roughly thatched with straw and turf.

The walls resembled an old dry stone dyke, while a hole in the top did duty for a chimney. There was a sickly odour of peat reek hanging about them. They seemed to be built anywhere, and sometimes you would find in a damp hollow quite a cluster of them forming a township. I was glad, however, to see on my last visit that many of these huts were much improved, and a great many new ones had been built on higher and dryer ground. It is only by coming in contact with the islanders and seeing their homes that one can realize the inconveniences to which they are subjected, and the strange isolated life they lead. Some hard things have been said about the crofters, sometimes by people living in luxury in our modern towns, who have never even seen the Hebrides, people who are not in a position to judge, but who are always ready to do so. Do not let us be too hard on the crofters, for they have been born and brought up to a primitive kind of life, and it must be a terrible wrench to them when they have to emigrate, as hundreds have had to do of late. There is one thing certain, they will never forget " the lone shieling of the misty island."

After leaving Castle Bay we passed a succession of small islands, the most important being Eriskay, famous in Jacobite lore. On 23rd July, 1745, Prince Charlie landed here from the *Doutelle* and met the chiefs of Boisdale and Clanranald, vainly soliciting their aid in the rising he had come to lead.

The long range of steep gneissic cliffs that stretch along the coast now lay before us. South Uist, Benbecula, and North Uist consist mainly of a maze of promontories, lochs, bogs and channels. As you

enter the harbour at Loch Boisdale you are again reminded of the fishing industry by the enormous
number of herring barrels stacked up on the pier.
There is a first class hotel, which is much frequented
by anglers, for there is plenty of both sea and loch
fishing to be had there.

We entered Loch Uskevagh as the shades of night
were falling. Just as I was gazing up the loch, in
the dim twilight a four-oared boat with a lug sail
came into sight. It required a very little stretch of
imagination in such a romantic spot to see Flora
Macdonald and " Betty Burke " sitting in the stern.
It was on the north side of this loch and near Rossen-
ish that Prince Charlie donned the female attire, and,
as Betty Burke, sailed down the loch with Flora
Macdonald just as the dusk was falling, on their
adventurous voyage to Skye.

Loch Eport in North Uist is one of the loveliest
lochs in the Outer Hebrides, and we left it just as the
last rays of the sun were kissing a distant hilltop and
the gulls were searching for their evening meal.
It has a very narrow entrance, and is guarded by many
rocks, which make navigation difficult. It almost
intersects the island from east to west, and is, roughly
speaking, in a straight line about eight miles long.
Of course it branches off in almost every direction
and its surface is dotted with a great number of little
islands, which seem to scintillate in the sunshine
like opals in an emerald sea. In earlier times it was a
great resort of smugglers but the natives have now
settled down to a less exciting occupation, that of
gathering kelp, from which iodine and other chemicals
are extracted.

CASTLEBAY, BARRA.

We had not time to do justice to this beautiful loch, for I had promised my friend, the minister at Loch Maddy, to call on him that day to get some messages to take out to St. Kilda, where for three years he had been the minister.

We arrived at Loch Maddy late in the afternoon. We had little time to spend there, however, as we wished to get to St. Kilda early the next morning and had to navigate the Sound of Harris before darkness fell. The Sound is the gateway to St. Kilda, and here we bade adieu to the Outer Hebrides.

The west coast of Scotland is a delightful centre for the study of wild bird life, for in sailing about amongst the islands all kinds of sea birds are constantly coming under notice ; some are perched on the high cliffs and some on shelving rock, while others are peacefully enjoying themselves swimming about on the water. It is undoubtedly a nursery of wild fowl, and the naturalist has every opportunity of studying them in their native haunts. A few weeks spent amongst the islands are both healthful and invigorating and always productive of delightful and lingering memories.

CHAPTER XII.

A LONELY WESTERN OUTPOST— ST. KILDA.

"Far in the western seas there lies an isle
Sport of the waves, lashed with an angry roar."

LIKE a sentry on outpost duty, guarding the Outer Hebrides, stands the lonely island of St. Kilda in the midst of the tempestuous waves of the Atlantic. It lies about fifty miles nearly due west of the Sound of Harris. With the exception of the occasional visit of a trawler, all communication with the mainland is practically cut off from September to May, and it is only during the summer months that an attempt can be made to reach the island, and even then, in stormy weather, boats have sometimes to return without being able to effect a landing.

St. Kilda is popularly known as a small island standing alone, but this is not so—there is, strictly speaking, a group ; two large islands, St. Kilda and Soay, and two smaller ones, Boreray and Dun, with several small adjacent stacs. However, St. Kilda, or as the natives prefer to call it, Hirta, is the only one inhabited.* It has three distinctive peaks ranged in a semi-circle around the village bay—Oiseval, Conachair, and Mullach Mor. The highest peak is

---

*This chapter and the two following were written before the evacuation of the island in 1930. In Chapter XV this event is described.

Conachair, and behind it lie the famous cliffs. Hirta is two and a half miles long and one and three quarters broad, but a very little part of its surface is available for grazing or cultivation. It is rough and stony and great boulders lie about everywhere. There are no cattle, sheep or horses on the island, and the dogs are a mongrel breed of collie. When Martin, who was amongst the first writers on St. Kilda, visited the island in 1697, he records that there were eighteen horses there. The Soay sheep are of the old St. Kilda breed. Their wool, which is dark brown, brings about twice the price of that of the other sheep. It is a difficult matter to say who first owned St. Kilda, as records on this subject are very complicated and difficult to follow. There is some record of a charter having been granted by the Lord of the Isles to his son, Reginald, about the middle of the fourteenth century, and it is said to have been confirmed by King Robert II. It now belongs to the Macleods, however, who have been in possession for centuries, and as they are presumed to be descendants of the Kings of Man, who are credited by tradition with the ownership of the islands, the group may have been in their possession all through the dim ages.

There is no doubt that St. Kilda must have been inhabited long before the fourteenth century, though there is no record of the people who first lived on the island or of how they reached it, other than the whimsical story of an Irishman named M'Queen having been the first to set foot on it. This legend may have arisen from the fact that the name was very common on the island, and, indeed, still is.

There are the ruins of some underground houses,

and in one of these, where excavations were made a considerable number of years ago, there were found some earthenware dishes and spear heads all more or less well preserved and identified as belonging to the Viking age. This would almost suggest that St. Kilda was inhabited over a thousand years ago. On the other hand, it is rather remarkable that the style of these underground houses is not that usually adopted by the Vikings, so that one would almost think that these houses must have been built by the St. Kildan aborigines, and been taken possession of by the Norwegian pirates after some of their fights. The houses are something after the fashion of the ancient Pictish houses found in some parts of the Hebrides. They are all as a rule very small with the exception of the one known as the "Female Warrior's" house, which was of much larger dimensions. The only sleeping accommodation seems to have been little hollow chambers in the walls, which were of enormous thickness.

At one time there was a circle of stones on Boreray and one on Soay, which would point to the existence of Druids at some period. At some places there were also found relics of ancient altars like those used in pagan times. There is, too, an old wall extending across the eastern end of Dun which may have given the island its name. Dun means a fort, and though there are no traces of a fort visible now, in the early days it may have been connected with St. Kilda and have formed a part of the island. In this case it is not at all improbable that this little island, which overlooks the village bay and is only disconnected from the main island by a narrow channel, was used

EVENING ON LOCH EPORT, NORTH UIST.

The gulls were searching for their evening meal.

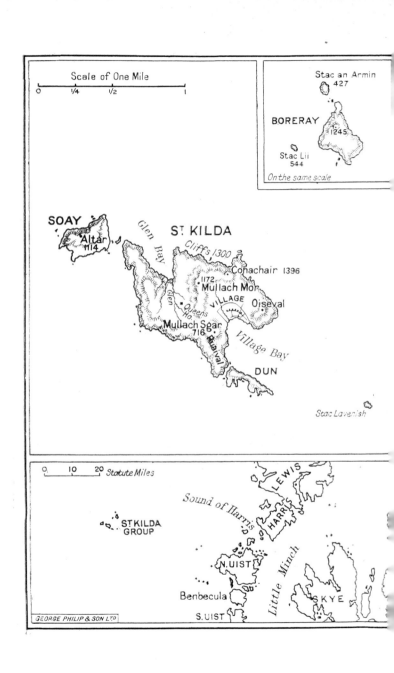

Scale of One Mile

0   1/4   1/2   1

Stac an Armin
427

BORERAY
1245

Stac Lii
544

On the same scale

SOAY
Altar
114

Glen Bay

Glen

Queens Ho

ST. KILDA

Cliffs 1300

Conachair 1396

1172
Mullach Mor

Oiseval

VILLAGE

Mullach Sgar
716

Ruaival

Village Bay

DUN

Stac Lavenish

0   10   20 Statute Miles

LEWIS

Sound of Harris

HARRIS

ST KILDA
GROUP

N.UIST

Little Minch

Benbecula

SKYE

GEORGE PHILIP & SON LTD

S.UIST

as a kind of watch-tower against the invasions of the Vikings.

One can only conjecture as to who were the original inhabitants, but it is a generally accepted theory now that the present inhabitants are not descended from them.

Nearly all the islands forming the St. Kilda group are pretty much alike in their formation—a kind of grassy tableland sloping towards the cliffs or precipices. Any one arriving at St. Kilda could not help being struck with the bold aspect of these bluff crags which rise sheer out of the water. With the exception of the village bay there is really no landing place on any of the islands that does not entail a dangerous climb. The black frowning cliffs rise out of the angry seething waves with a stern threatening look which seems to augur destruction to any boat that may be dashed against them. The coast of Skye is said to be one of the boldest in Scotland, but for wild grandeur and impressive cliff scenery, Skye must take second place to St. Kilda.

Some of the lichen-covered caves around the coast are also very fine and look as if they had been painted a variety of striking colours, while the sand and sea-weed at the bottom produce some marvellous colour effects on the water, and you find anything at times from deep mauve to a pale emerald. It is only safe to enter the caves in calm weather, though the St. Kildans have sometimes to remain in them a whole night during a storm. When this is the case a religious service is always held, for every St. Kildan youth can repeat a chapter of the Bible and say a prayer and lead the praise.

H

Conachair, the highest hill on the island, rises boldly to the height of 1,396 feet. From this point it looks as if some mighty giant in early days had cut the island in two, thrown the northern half into the sea and left the present St. Kilda standing. From this peak there is a slope of about seventy feet, terminating in the famous cliffs, with a sheer drop of practically thirteen hundred feet into the seething Atlantic.

The general view of St. Kilda as seen from the bay appears to be one long rough grassy slope to the top of Conachair, strewn with huge boulders, and this is really the case so far, but once you have climbed up these rugged slopes, an altogether different view meets the eye. Instead of a continuation of rough and uninteresting rock-covered pasture, the blue Atlantic stretches away to the horizon, while to the east, on a clear day, the dim outline of Lewis can be seen. But the most wonderful sight of all is that which is to be seen below. The roar of the Atlantic as it beats against the foot of the cliffs can only be heard indistinctly ; for once in a way it has to take second place to the scream of the seabirds. Every little peak and jutting crag is crowded with fulmars and puffins, while hundreds of feet below the air is a seething mass of seabirds of every kind, sailing hither and thither, some giving vent to shrill notes and others to plaintive cries. Now and then the hoarse croak of the raven can also be heard, along with the ceaseless call of " kitt-i-wake " from the pretty little gull of that name, and the sharp " wheep wheep " of the oyster-catcher. Far below, the sea and rocks are only seen at intervals, and even then indistinctly, as they are constantly blurred by interwoven meshes of dull grey, white or brown, relieved every here and there with streaks of orange, black and red, as the puffin or the oyster-catcher flashes past.

The scenery of St. Kilda is by no means what one would call beautiful. There is nothing about it that resembles our Highland scenery. It is wild in the extreme and awe-inspiring, as you look up at those dark beetling cliffs and hear the angry roar of the Atlantic echoing and re-echoing amongst the many caves.

The house is still shown which the unfortunate Lady Grange occupied when she was imprisoned on the island in 1734. It is of the old beehive pattern and is now used as a cleit to store turf in for the winter fuel. Lady Grange was the wife of one of the Lords of Council and Session who, finding that he had no further use for her, had her secretly conveyed to this remote prison house, and not only informed the world at large that she was dead but actually carried out the funeral rites. She remained on the island for six years and her solitary life there must have been a living death.

At one time St. Kilda seems to have been joined to the island of Harris, if we can believe tradition, for there is no historical record of that period. There is a story, however, current amongst the natives that a certain woman, known as the " Warrior Queen," had permission to hunt on the lands betwen Hirta and Harris, and there is a deep ravine in the island known as the " Female Warrior's Glen." When Martin visited the island he was shown a pair of antlers which had been dug out of Oiseval, the hill to the east of the village, and the old house was also pointed out to him where the warrior queen was said to have lived. It was situated at the foot of the glen near the Well of Virtues.

The bay can only be entered in calm weather or with certain favourable winds. When the wind blows hard from the south-east and a heavy sea is running, a boat is in great danger of being carried on the rocks.

The climate is fairly mild for the situation of the island, but it has a tendency, as one would expect, to be humid, particularly when there are south-west winds blowing, and consequently rheumatism is very prevalent. Several years ago, however, in the late autumn it was so hot and dry that every blade of grass on the hills was scorched brown and the face of Conachair was so slippery that one could scarcely reach the top. But if the ascent was bad, the descent was much worse, and one had to resort to the expedient of sitting down, trusting to Providence and tobogganing to the bottom. Arriving there you might discover to your horror, as I did, that you were badly in want of a needle and thread.

That was one of the most memorable visits I ever paid to the lonely isle. We got safely through the Sound of Harris just before dusk, and sailed out under a full moon and over a calm sea. When I say "calm" I do not wish any one to treat the word literally, for you never really get it calm crossing those fifty miles. We passed Stac Lavenish gleaming under the powerful searchlight of the midnight heavens, and a few minutes later when we arrived in the bay, it had a distinctly weird and uncanny look and made one think of Tir-nan-Og. The full moon seemed to shine above in a greater glory than it had ever done before, and the high lights on the water were like burnished silver,

CHURCH, SCHOOL AND MANSE, ST. KILDA.

while the three peaks of Oiseval, Conachair and Mullach Mor, forming a kind of crescent, loomed up like ghostly giants from shadowland. Every shadow was intensely black—so were the cliffs. A strange uneasy feeling seemed to be in the air as if spirits were abroad and lurking in the depths of that awful gloom.

In the darkness one could only conjecture the position of the little village on the high ground by a steady light shining from one of the houses, where, doubtless, some sick person lay. The silence was awful, but was at times relieved by the deep booming of the sea in a cave which seemed to be somewhere in the black depths of Ruaival. There were three of us standing on the deck of the little boat in this ghostly moonlight and we each looked deadly pale, and never spoke—we seemed phantoms on a phantom ship. I can see the scene as I write, just as I saw it then, in the queer filmy shimmer of that early autumn morning.

It must be a wonderful sight to see a storm breaking on St. Kilda, just such a one as I experienced some years ago in trying to reach the island. We were caught about ten miles out from the Sound of Harris, just as darkness set in, and all night long we were the plaything of the storm, with an inky black sky overhead, the wind howling like ten thousand demons let loose, and the rain, spray and waves dashing continually over us. Daylight was a welcome sight, and when it came we were back in the Sound of Harris. We were presumed to have been about five miles from the islands, which were smothered up in clouds of spindrift and seething breakers. It would have been utterly impossible to attempt a landing, and only courting disaster to risk venturing nearer in such a sea, so we were compelled to return without paying our respects to lone St. Kilda.

The church, school and manse, all of the most primitive kind, stand on the high ground above the bay, while a little farther along is the post office and factor's house. A further walk through the tangled weeds and grass—for you could not with any degree of accuracy call it a road—brings you to the little village, which consists of sixteen houses built in a semi-circle. They were erected about the year 1863. Some of the old houses are still to be seen adjacent to the present ones. The houses are substantially built of stone and lime and are about eight feet high, with corrugated iron roofs, whitewashed and some of them quite neat and tidy, while others could be better cared for. There are many houses both in the Outer and Inner Hebrides that are in a much more squalid condition than those on St. Kilda.

Soay lies to the north-west and is only separated from St. Kilda by a channel about a quarter of a mile in breadth. Its highest point is near the western side, where it rises a little over twelve hundred feet. There is no landing place in the island and you have just to leap to a slanting rock when the boat rises on a wave, a feat which is both difficult and dangerous to any but a St. Kildan. The island has some good pasture and there are several hundred of the old St. Kildan breed of sheep kept there. They are curious looking creatures and very wild, and remind one of badly shaped and stunted deer. They are very nimble and sure-footed and you will find them climbing amongst some of the most dangerous crags with no apparent fear and far from the reach of any one.

Boreray lies to the north-east of St. Kilda and is about four miles distant. It is a little higher than Soay and has also no landing place but a dangerous climb up a steep and slippery rock face. It consists of a series of serrated ridges and peaks covered with thousands upon thousands of sea birds of all kinds. It would be difficult to exaggerate the number of these birds, and it is quite a sight to see them rise in their countless myriads. They almost obscure the sky and suggest the flakes of a great snowstorm fluttering in mid-air. There are also sheep on Boreray, and when the fowling and wool-plucking season came round a little band used to leave St. Kilda for the island where they often remained for a week or ten days at a time. Their beds were often a hole in the ground or a crevice in the rocks. A woman went with the expedition to prepare the meals, and should they be compelled to remain over a Sunday an elder often accompanied them to hold divine worship, for the average St. Kildan would not rest in his grave if he missed one Sunday service. Things, however, have changed and they rarely go for more than one night to catch gannets in the spring, while in the summer time they go for a week to pluck the wool from the sheep. They have little turf huts erected now where they sleep.

There are a great number of stacs of the most fantastic description dotted all around, some of them rising out of the water like great needles and reaching a height of six hundred feet. They are all more or less the abode of sea birds which keep circling around them, apparently in some cases scarcely able to get a foothold. Stac an Armin is a striking example. It rises with a rounded hump to a sharp point over six hundred feet above the sea, then drops to the water in the form of a half-moon. Stac Lii is perhaps the best known because it is the chosen home of the gannets, and looking across from the top of Conachair on a sunny day it looks as if it were painted white, so thickly is it tenanted by the solan geese. Stac Lavenish is also well known because it seems to guard the entrance to the village bay and has been selected by the great black-backed gulls as their home.

Few people who have not seen St. Kilda can realize what it is like. How often people ask if there are any shops or hotels in the place. One accustomed to busy life in a city cannot realize a place where the sound of a locomotive has never been heard, where there is no inn or hotel, where there is no such thing as a road, not even from the houses to the landing slip at the rocks, but merely a narrow path through the dock weeds and tangled grass, where there is no doctor or policeman ; a place more or less cut off from all outside communication from September to May— yet such a place is the Lonely Isle.

We said farewell to the island in brilliant sunshine. To me there was a touch of sadness in that farewell. I had just said good-bye to my friend, Donald Gillies, never dreaming then that I was so soon to hear of his tragic death of acute appendicitis on the Island of Boreray during a wool-plucking expedition. He was a stalwart son of the Hebrides, bold and fearless on the cliffs and a fine sailor.

We sailed slowly down the bay with the gulls screaming around us while the little band stood on the rocks waving their hands.   Little did they know then what the future had in store for them.

CHAPTER XIII.

ST. KILDA—THE PEOPLE.

" All the men are magnificent climbers, and I would
trust myself on any cliff with a St. Kildan for my
guide."—*Pike*.

AS you pass Stac Lavenish and arrive off the bay,
the row of little houses which comprises the
village is scarcely discernible against the rough and
stony background which forms the base of Conachair,
and the island seems deserted.

The echo of the ship's whistle or bell soon resounds
amongst the rocks and caves, and as you sail up the
bay and drop anchor the dogs, like angry demons,
come rushing down to the rocks and give you a real
St. Kilda greeting. A few more applications of the
whistle or bell and the St. Kildans, who are never in
a hurry, begin to make their appearance and walk
down in a very leisurely fashion to the landing slip.
After a lot of noise and unnecessary talk in Gaelic a
boat is launched, and they push off just to see what
they can do for you. Another long discussion ensues,
in a mixture of Gaelic and English, and then you get
into their boat and are rowed to the landing place.
This is just a little concrete slip jutting out from a
sheltered rock. At one time there was no landing
place—you had just to wait until the boat rose on a
wave and leap on to a tangle-covered rock, taking your
chance of arriving safely; the odds were all in favour
of your slipping and falling back into the water—quite

a usual occurrence—but luckily the bay is very shallow at that part.

The natives are generally arranged in two groups to meet you—the men on the one side, and the women on the other. You are greeted with a friendly shaking of hands, and as they are very fond of confections of all kinds, any little presents of tobacco or sweetmeats are gratefully received by them.

When I first went out in 1903 the men were dressed on week days in rough homespun trousers, very baggy and just a shade neater than those adopted by a famous English University, a sleeved waistcoat, and a thick red muffler twisted as a rule twice round the throat.

The women were much more picturesque than the men, and while the men both wove and made their own clothes, they were also designers and dressmakers for the ladies and seemed to display greater variety and ingenuity in their department. The women wore a coarse blue and red striped skirt or petticoat cut short to the knee, and a kind of loose jacket. The unmarried girls had a gay kerchief of many colours tied over their heads, while the married women wore a neat white snood, which is the coveted badge of wifehood in the island. Some of the younger women wore stockings and boots, but few of the elder women did so.

Things, however, have changed very much since then, and in many respects the people have become wonderfully modern, and this is particularly noticeable in their Sunday dress. The young men now appear in well-cut dark tweed suits, with collar and tie. Some of the women even wear hats. Others still seem to prefer the gay kerchief, and the older women still keep to the original style, and they only wear thick woollen stockings and no boots.

The St. Kildans are rather clumsy in their gait and consequently have a lazy look. They are never in the least hurry; this undoubtedly is due to the fact that they have no fixed occupation, and time is no object to them. What they cannot get through to-day will do quite well to-morrow, and they have no mails to catch, nor anything to hurry them. Still the St. Kildan is not to be despised. During the winter he works hard weaving and making clothes. He is also a man who can endure hardships if need be, and taking all into account his life is not a bed of roses. He is one of the finest cragsmen in the world and faithful to the last on the cliffs. If you are an ornithologist and desirous of working on the cliffs you can safely place your life in his hands and it will be no fault of his if he fails you. Boys under sixteen are not allowed to go fowling on any dangerous part of the cliffs but are taken up for practice and to accustom them to the work. The men are bold and fearless while " walking " down the face of a cliff on the rope and there are few accidents considering the dangerous nature of the work.

Every one has heard of the St. Kilda Parliament. It is a quaint institution and meets daily shortly after breakfast. They have no glorified Westminster to meet in but assemble in the open air in front of the post office, with the canopy of heaven for a roof. There they discuss the affairs of the island and the work that is to be done for the day. Some of the members sit in a row on stones along the front of the

ST. KILDA WOMAN AND CHILDREN.

building while some of the younger ones squat on the ground or stand. The dogs prowl about in the rear, or Strangers' Gallery. The affairs of this little world are discussed in the mother tongue—Gaelic. When trouble arises and they cannot agree about what is to be done for the day they adjourn for the midday meal, and that means that nothing in particular will be done at all. But should they feel in a working mood, then the session is dismissed early and all are alert and set to work with a will until the job is finished. There is no prime minister and no speaker, but each joins in the general discussion just as the spirit moves him.

One of the most remarkable things connected with the island was a disease amongst the children known as Infantile Lockjaw or " eight days' sickness." It was roughly estimated that about three-fourths of the children born died before they were eight days old. There were several scientific conjectures given as to the cause of this awful mortality, which extended for over a century. Nothing, however, seemed to have been definitely decided, and to show the uncertainty with which a woman regarded the life of her child, she rarely provided any clothing until the eight days had passed. The entire lack of knowledge of the proper feeding and keeping of a child at that age was put forward as one of the reasons, and so convinced were some of this that a trained nurse was sent out, and since then the death rate has fallen and the disease has almost disappeared.

Macaulay in 1758 took notice of this strange disease, and the symptoms then seemed to be much the same as they were at a more recent date.   About the fourth or fifth day after the child was born it lost all power of suction and on the seventh its gums became so paralysed that nothing could be got down its throat.   It was then seized with convulsions, and after suffering much, died of sheer exhaustion on the eighth day.   Many doctors have given their opinion of the cause of this dreadful disease, but as they more or less differed, the matter resolved itself into speculation.

At one time there was a disease amongst the children of Ireland of a similar kind, known as " nine day fits." A large percentage of the children born died of this disease, and it was generally ascribed at that time to the presence of a vitiated atmosphere.   On this being remedied the death rate was much lower—and consequently many came to the conclusion that this was the cause of the disease on St. Kilda.   On the other hand, some ascribed it to intermarriage, some to an entire lack of midwifery skill, and others to a want of attention and proper food both for the mother and child. Some were agreed that the consanguinity question had a good deal to do with it, but it may be pointed out that such consequences of consanguineous marriages as insanity, imbecility and deaf-mutism were entirely absent.

When Mr Fiddes was minister on the island he was untiring in his efforts to investigate the causes of the disease and consulted doctors in Glasgow on the subject, with the result that the disease has practically been stamped out.   Miss Maclean, daughter of the minister, wrote me on Christmas Day, 1912, that not a single child during her three years' stay on the island had died from this cause.

Everything on St. Kilda in this respect has made a marked advance, and both housing, feeding and nursing are much better than they used to be. While there is still no doctor there is a nurse on the island, and this lifts a grave responsibility off the shoulders of the minister, who was in a sense responsible for the physical well-being of his flock.

The population of St. Kilda seems to have fluctuated very much, but the cause in unknown. About the year 1830 there were just over a hundred inhabitants. Since then the population has gradually decreased, and at the present day it is a little under half that number.

An early instance of the depopulation of the place is recorded in 1729 when an epidemic of smallpox brought by a boat practically swept the island of its inhabitants. A few, however, were on Boreray at the time. There is no place about Boreray where a boat can be left and the custom is for the boatman to land those who are to stay and return for them on a given day. The boat bringing the epidemic arrived in their absence with the consequence that all on the island were stricken down and there was no one left to take them off for several months. Those left on Boreray had no way of knowing why they had been deserted, and amongst a race of people who are so faithful to each other their life during these months must have been a trying one.

With the exception of a period from about 1830 to 1843, when the Rev. Neil Mackenzie kept a record, no proper register of births, deaths and marriages was kept, until in 1856 the Registrar-General took the matter in hand.

The chief diet of the St. Kildans is boiled fulmars, puffins, solan geese, mutton, oatmeal, eggs and potatoes when they can get them, but the latter are rather scarce. Porridge and tea also form part of the diet. This at first sight seems quite sumptuous fare, but when you take into account the tough nature of some of the sea-birds' flesh, the entire lack of variety in the food, and the want of vegetables, it is not to be wondered at that dyspepsia is a common complaint on the island. Potatoes are the only vegetable they have and the island only produces a supply to last a very short time. Sometimes a trawler arriving in the bay may leave them some provisions, but they are often at starvation's door long before the boat from Glasgow is due in the spring to bring them a fresh supply of food.

Considering the great risk in working on the cliffs during the fowling period, accidents are comparatively few. There have been, of course, some very serious ones. Only a few years ago two of the men, Ewen Gillies and John M'Donald, went down the cliffs to catch young fulmars. They were roped together but one fell and took the other with him. The rope seems to have broken or been cut on some jagged ledge, for one of the bodies was recovered from a cleft, but the other was never found, having fallen into the relentless sea that is always waiting to claim its victims.

Some writers, among them some who have never visited the islands, have said hard things against the St. Kildans. But whatever may be said against them, they are at heart a kindly disposed people, who mean

Two Old Crones, St. Kilda.

well, and while you are with them you are one of them. They are extremely solicitous for your welfare ; indeed, those who have lived for some time in their midst say that it is almost embarrassing when they call each morning to ask if you are well, if you have had a good night's sleep, and if they can do anything for you.

The only events of importance that make a stir in their monotonous lives are the first appearance of the sea-birds in spring, and the arrival of the first boat from Glasgow with food in May. As the island is quite out of the route of all traffic, occasional whalers or trawlers are the only boats seen at very rare intervals, and these can only enter the bay if the weather is favourable, so that all the St. Kildan has for a little diversion during the winter months is to watch the playful Atlantic pitting its strength against his rock-bound home.

The St. Kildans have always been noted for their zeal for religion and religious services. As far back as one can trace this has been so. They are very strict about Sabbath observance, and will do little that savours of the secular on that day. Though they should be practically starving, and a boat arrive with provisions late on Saturday night, they would stop getting the food ashore at midnight, and not begin unloading again until twelve o'clock on Monday morning. This is no doubt due to the teaching of some of their early advisers, and its effect has come down through generations to the present inhabitants. They are not now nearly so strict in this respect as they used to be, but still some of the old inherited ideas die hard.

I

The early St. Kildans had certainly some quaint observances on Sunday. After breakfast they prepared for church, though they did not know exactly when the service would begin. The minister was usually timekeeper on the island, so they patiently waited until the first tinkle of the bell, then every door seemed to swing open as if by one action and out streamed the men, women and children, and walked along the narrow path to the church—the two sexes separately.

When Sands visited the island about half a century ago he made some very scathing remarks about the Sabbath observances. He said it was a day of intolerable gloom, and that the people hurried to the church neither looking to the right nor the left, for that was considered sinful, and that they looked like a troop of the damned being driven to the bottomless pit. If Sands was correct in his statement, then things must have changed very much for the better, for apart from the fact that they will do no work on Sunday, I saw no trace of this wretched state of affairs. They walked to the church in a leisurely fashion like rational beings. When the service was over I photographed them leaving the church, and instead of scowls I only received smiles, and no one objected in the least. On Sunday afternoon Christiana M'Queen, daughter of Finlay M'Queen, the famous cragsman, along with another St. Kildan, spent several hours on the top of Conachair with me, pointing out various peculiarities in the fulmars. She also described the methods of descending the cliffs and pointed out a ledge far below where her father had rested and adjusted his load before ascending the face of a dangerous precipice. She was a most interesting guide and I could not have wished for a better, and all this happened on a Sunday afternoon.

The church bell hangs on a frail wooden erection outside the church door, and on close inspection is seen to bear the inscription " Janet Cowan, 1861." Naturally one would conclude that this generous-minded lady had presented the bell. But no such thing ; " Janet Cowan " was a boat wrecked on the rocks, and the St. Kildans appropriated the bell and hung it there to call them to their many religious duties.

Christianity seems to have been introduced into the island at an early date. One of the chapels in existence in 1697 was dedicated to St. Bredan, an Irish saint who spent some time amongst the western islands in the early centuries, and it is just possible that he reached St. Kilda, though how or when seems unknown. Another was dedicated to St. Columba, which would almost lead one to believe that the monks of Iona had also had a hand in the proselytizing of the early St. Kildans.

Although there were three chapels on the island when Martin visited them at the end of the seventeenth century, the St. Kildans seem to have been left to do pretty much as they liked so far as religion was concerned. A minister only called at intervals to marry and baptize, and when he neglected his duty the people performed these rites themselves to the best of their ability, and doubtless to their own satisfaction. The Reverend Alex. Buchan was their first permanent minister. He remained with them from 1705 until he died in 1729.

It is not to be wondered at that St. Kilda was so long without a minister of religion. The life on the island at the present time is lonely enough, but in those days it must have meant banishment to a well educated man. There was another very important point to be considered : the salary then paid, somewhere under £20, could not be called by any means tempting, and so long as it remained at about that figure there was little chance for the St. Kildans. Why Mr. Buchan remained so long is a mystery, but doubtless he was actuated by a sense of duty.

About 1830 the little church and manse were erected, and the salary was fixed at £50. Dr. Mac-Donald, " the Apostle of the North," took a great interest in the island and paid several visits there between 1822 and 1830. On his first visit he said that he did not find a single man who could be called a religious person. He said nothing about the women. Perhaps he found them spiritually better, or, seeing that he did not record such a fact, perhaps he was a gallant gentleman and refrained from remarking about them. He certainly set about his duties with a will, and if constant exercise in religious affairs makes a Christian, then the St. Kildans must have reached a state of absolute perfection, for he held a meeting for two hours every morning and the same again at night; and apart from these meetings he made it a point to examine them individually as he met them during the day.

The Rev. Neil M'Kenzie was on the island from 1830 to 1843. He was quite a different type of man and did a great deal of good. He did his utmost to

St. Kilda.
The Village and Oiseval.

improve the condition of the people, and tried to introduce an elementary form of education.

The next minister, Mr. Mackay, missed a glorious opportunity of continuing the good work begun by Mr M'Kenzie. He seemed to prefer to take a leaf out of Dr. MacDonald's book, but he completely outshone the " apostle." He started his reign of terror in 1865 and never once left his flock during his long stay on the island. He remained monarch of all he surveyed for twenty-five years. Sabbath observance was a strong point with Mr. Mackay, and woe betide the man who dared to speak above his breath or look happy on that day! Excommunication was his punishment for sleeping in church, and to such an extent did he carry his notions that water was not allowed to be drawn on Sunday. Weekdays were much the same, for the people were taught to look upon such harmless amusements as athletics, whistling, games or dancing as abominations in the eyes of the Lord.

Mr. Mackay completely ruled the island with an iron hand and a great many of the ridiculous notions of the St. Kildans are due to his teaching. He kept the people completely under his thumb, and no one dared to contradict him. Mr. Connell tells a very amusing story of a Sunday he spent on the island in October, 1885. His landlady, as he calls her, offered him for his morning ablutions a basin with no more than a pint of water in it. On this fact being pointed out to the good dame she explained, " It's the Sabbath," and informed him of the minister's prohibition against the drawing of water on that day. Mr. Connell says that, on hearing this, he was not disposed to invoke a blessing on the head of Mr. Mackay, and proposed that he himself should break the Sabbath.   On hearing this the good old soul, who was not a native of the island, with a comic twinkle in her eye pointed to a pitcher of water, newly drawn from the well and hidden away behind the door, saying, " It's no alloot, but whiles we draw a wee drap on the sly."

As mentioned before, the minister was time-keeper on the island, and Mr. Mackay used to boast that he liked to be about two hours in advance of the world in this respect.   Things, however, changed for the better under the care of Mr. Fiddes, who did a great deal for the island and the people, and encouraged progress in every respect.   He was a broadminded man who worked hard to brighten up their drab existence, and it was he who succeeded in practically rooting out the dreadful scourge of " eight days' sickness."

The religious welfare of the island is at present cared for by Mr. M'Leod, the missionary, who is doing his best to uphold the traditions of his more recent predecessors ; and the affairs of the flesh are in the capable hands of an experienced nurse, so that there is progress even on remote St. Kilda.

CHAPTER XIV.

ST. KILDA—BIRD LIFE ON THE CLIFFS.

" Hushed be thy moaning, lone bird of the sea ;
Thy home on the rocks is a shelter to thee."

ST. KILDA is perhaps one of the best of our
ornithological stations, but, curiously enough,
there are many people who visit the lonely isle and
return having seen scarcely a sea bird about the place.
Occasionally there are a few gulls flying overhead,
and sometimes the great black-backed gulls come in
from Lavenish to do some scavenging around the bay,
while at intervals the solan geese, getting tired of
their ordinary haunts at Stac Lii, come over to fish.
With these exceptions there are few sea birds to be
seen near the village.

There are myriads of birds on the island, however,
though many may not have seen them. The reason
is not far to seek. So far as St. Kilda is concerned,
they are all located on the cliffs of Conachair behind
the village, and before you can see them in their
native haunts you have a very arduous and steep climb
of 1396 feet. Unless you go up the valley between
Conachair and Mullach Mor to a point on the coast
line called Gob-na-Airde there is no other way of
seeing the cliffs from the land than by making this
steep ascent. On reaching the top you will find that
the cliffs are simply white with seabirds ; every ridge
and peak is covered with them, while thousands are
sailing silently backwards and forwards between you

and the water. Picture these cliffs fully half a mile long covered with birds, and you will have a slight idea of the numbers at St. Kilda alone, for there are also the adjacent islands of Soay, Boreray and the Dun, Stac Lii, Stac Armin and many smaller stacs.

Most of those who visit the island do not take the trouble to climb, and are all unconscious of the delightful view to be had from the top, apart from the interesting sight of the birds.

There are about eleven different kinds of sea birds to be found on the island—gannets, petrels, gulls, guillemots, razorbills, puffins, cormorants, oystercatchers, dunlins and ducks. There are also some eight or nine different kinds of land birds, but as a number of these are well known it is only necessary to mention a few of the rarer visitors, and the wren which is peculiar to the island.

Of all the sea birds the most majestic and imposing is the gannet or solan goose. Gannets are purely local birds, and with their quaint habits and the very human way they sit and look at you, they make a very interesting study. They are rarely found in towards the shore, preferring to keep well out to sea when they are not at their nesting stations. The principal stations in Scotland are the Bass Rock, Ailsa Craig and Stac Lii at St. Kilda. The nearest I have ever seen them to the coast in any numbers was once at the Mull of Kintyre, where hundreds were fishing close to the shore, but I saw none venture inland, and when they seemed tired of their amusement they betook themselves back to their beloved rock.

The length of the gannet is about thirty-four inches

and its beak is about six inches long.   The skin of the face and neck, which is generally devoid of feathers, is of a pale bluish colour, the eye is light hazel and the legs and web black.   The feathers of the head and neck are of a creamy white, some of them almost yellow, whilst the body tends towards white.   The wing primaries are in striking contrast, being jet black.   Once seen no one could mistake the gannet on the wing.   Its flight seems very slow, though in reality the bird gets along at a great speed.   It seems strangely shaped in flight, and bears little or no resemblance to the well-proportioned bird it looks when seen sitting on a ledge of rock.   When in flight the neck is well extended with head and beak slightly drooping ;   the long wings seem then placed far back, and the whole appearance, combined with a short tail, gives the bird a curious but striking and imposing look.   The young birds when hatched are almost black and naked, but very soon assume a white, downy covering all over.   They then pass through several intermediate stages of brown until they assume their adult plumage, generally four or five years later.

The gannets' mode of flight is very different from that of other birds.   They give about half a dozen slow powerful beats of the wing, then soar, and repeat the wing beats again.   They will follow a ship for miles, apparently in search of food, though I never saw them take any.   They never seemed to associate in any way with the gulls, but always kept above, or on the fringe of the noisy crowd, not uttering a single sound, though the gulls were deafening at times. They look down with a kind of icy reserve as if they wish you thoroughly to understand that, though present, they have no connection with the vulgar crowd below.

It is a most interesting sight to see them fishing. I have watched them at various times, but never to such perfection as I saw them in front of the cliffs at Mullach Mor in St. Kilda Bay. They had come over in great numbers from Stac Lii, and were flitting to and fro in a most leisurely fashion, and quite oblivious to anything around them, so intent were they on watching for fish. Some were sailing just a little above the water, while others were anything from fifty to a hundred and fifty feet up. Their *modus operandi* is simple and interesting. They flit to and fro at a slow pace, then suddenly close their wings, and drop like a stone with a tremendous splash into the water. They are provided with a number of small sacs placed in the breast which they can inflate at will, thus breaking the impact when they strike the water. The sacs are also useful in making the bird more buoyant, and consequently help it to rise to the surface again quickly. I have seen them make a peculiar oblique dive from a great height. They dropped for about half the distance in the ordinary way—then turned over with extended wings, and in this position finished the plunge into the water, landing anything from thirty to fifty feet from their original course. When Martin visited the island over two hundred years ago he also took notice of this strange oblique dive. He used the word "asquint," and some ornithologists poked fun at his description and said all they liked about it was the word "asquint," but Martin was quite right in what he said.   Some birds rise just where they enter the water, while others rise from ten to twenty feet away or even further.   After wriggling the fish into position head first, they swallow it and are instantly on the wing again.

The nest is built on ledges of the rock, and is composed of seaweed, turf, moss or grass, sometimes in great quantities.   The gannet is a great thief, and has no hesitation in stealing from others while in search of material, with the result that many a battle royal is fought.   It lays one large egg of a slightly bluish colour, encrusted with lime, which soon becomes soiled during the process of incubation.

There are three petrels that frequent St. Kilda, the fulmar, the Manx shearwater, and Leach's forked-tailed petrel.   Fulmars are the birds principally associated with the island, because they remain there during the winter.   They generally leave for a month or so during the autumn to take the young birds for a tour round the coast, just to show them that there are other places than the lonely Isle, but they return in October and settle down for the winter.

The fulmar very much resembles a kittiwake gull at first sight, but I am afraid it would shock the pride of the fulmar were we to associate it with the gull tribe, for it looks like a bird that fancies itself very much, and undoubtedly looks with disdain on the little puffins that have taken up their abode on the cliffs adjacent to its home.   However, the puffin is quite capable of looking after itself, and when the fulmar sits up and throws out its chest in a way that it has, and looks across with disdain, doubtless the puffin thinks—you may consider yourself a fine-looking gentleman, but at least you have not a beak like mine ; and with his usual call of " ong-ong " he literally throws himself off the cliffs, flapping his short wings as he rushes about in great excitement, apparently challenging the fulmar to mortal combat. As the latter ignores him, however, he settles down on his cliff again quite contentedly.

The fulmars' chief nesting-place is St. Kilda and the adjacent stacs. Some are to be found on the cliffs of the mainland of Shetland, and on the lonely island of Foula, also on Unst, Bressay and Noss. Some nests have also been found on the Outer Hebrides, but they are not very common there. Fulmars have also been seen on the cliffs at Auchmithie near Arbroath, but in very small numbers.

The head, neck, breast, and tail of the fulmar are of a dingy white colour, the back and wings slate grey tipped with black, the head is rounded, and the neck seems short and thick, but it can be stretched out to a considerable length. It is very fond of sitting up and pursing out its breast like a pigeon. The bill is strong and large for the size of the bird, of a pale yellow colour, and with a peculiar cylinder above the upper mandible. Both upper and lower mandibles are hooked, and the tips seem as if they were separate pieces patched to the beak. The nostrils run along the lower part of the cylindrical portion of the upper mandible. The legs are dark brown and short. It lays one egg which very much resembles that of the gannet, and is white. It builds on the most inaccessible cliffs quite beyond the reach of the average person. It seems to prefer the top of a cliff covered with turf, where it scoops out a little

CONACHAIR, from the Bay, St. Kilda.

The highest peak is Conachair, and behind it lie the famous cliffs. The surface of the island is rough and stony and great boulders are lying about everywhere. A stone wall protects the few houses which form the village from falls of rock from Conachair. The cleits may be seen behind the houses, and two sheep corrals outside the wall.

round hole and deposits the egg.   Both male and
female take part in the process of incubation, which
lasts generally about six weeks, and it takes about the
same time before the young birds are able to fly.   The
young birds are considered a great delicacy by the
St. Kildans, and form their staple diet during the
winter months.   Each family keeps several barrels
of them salted.   The flesh is very white, being in the
old birds a mixture of fat and lean, while the young are
nearly all fat.

The fulmar's means of defence is an evil-smelling
oil which it can squirt in your face at will.   Luckily
its powers of discharging the oil are not great, as it
rarely reaches beyond three feet.   If, however,
it touches your clothes you may as well dispose of
them, for nothing will remove the offensive odour.
This oil is used by the St. Kildans, both commercially
and medicinally, and one bird usually contains about
half a pint.   It is not squirted through the tubular
nostril, as is generally supposed, but it is forced up
the throat, and through the mouth.   The fowler
has to be extremely careful when noosing the bird to
prevent it from bringing up the oil, but in this, of
course, the St. Kildan excels.   It is a fish oil, and is
said to possess nearly all the qualities of cod liver oil.

With their long wings fully extended the fulmars
sail backwards and forwards, scarcely a motion being
visible, and one can have nothing but admiration for
their graceful mode of flight.   When they leave the
cliffs they seem to be carried up on the breeze, higher
and higher they rise, then wheeling suddenly round
they soar back again as if thoroughly enjoying the
exhilarating motion.

If for nothing else, their extraordinary numbers entitle the puffins to consideration. They are such quaint and funny little birds, and so full of self-importance, fussiness and inquisitiveness that they would be sure to feel slighted if they did not get immediate attention. They greatly exceed all the other birds in number. They have a most comical appearance as they sit on the rocks with their little pudgy bodies and great beaks. The head is black, also the nape of the neck, and the whole of the upper parts, with a broad band around the throat which gives them the appearance of being in mourning. The under parts and breast are white and the legs a pretty orange colour. The enormously large beak is the extraordinary part of the bird and gives it a rather fantastic look. It reminds one of a Drury Lane mask, with its gay reds and yellows. The beak is very peculiarly shaped and is in reality only a sheath, parts of which are shed after the nesting season. It forms a sort of triangle, broad, short and very much compressed, and both mandibles are arched and traversely grooved. The ridge at the base is yellow, followed by a bluish colour, and three grooves of bright orange and red. The skin around the beak is also yellow, and the eye grey. The wings and tail are short, and consequently when it leaves the rocks it seems to hurl itself off and to have great difficulty in rising. Once on the wing it flies with great force, almost in a straight line and just above the water, but rarely goes far. The little webbed feet are spread out below its tail to act as a kind of rudder. When you scare the birds away they go in thousands, and so dense is their flight that if other birds get in their way there is a collision, and great excitement prevails. They are excellent divers and can swim for a long distance under water.

The puffin excavates a hole for its nest, or, better still, takes possession of a rabbit's warren. If the rightful owner cares to remain quiet—good and well ; but if it raises any objection then it is promptly evicted. The nest is sometimes composed of a few feathers or bits of grass, but often there is no attempt to make a nest at all. The puffin is one of those curious birds that we see a great deal of while it frequents our coasts, but little is known of its whereabouts after it has taken its departure. Its cool, persistent " cheek " has taken it all over the St. Kilda group. It is by no means timid, but is very inquisitive and some good photographs have been secured simply by patience and time.

The guillemots and razorbills are always to be found within measurable distance of each other and are so closely allied that I will speak of them together. At some distance it is difficult to distinguish the one bird from the other, as the head, neck and back of both are very dark, while the breast and underparts are white. The chief distinguishing feature is that the guillemot has a sharp pointed beak, which is much blacker than that of the razorbill, the latter having a rounded beak. It has also a white line running from the eye towards the base of the beak, while in the guillemot the line extends in a curve from the eye towards the back of the head. Their haunts are similar, both nesting on high precipitous cliffs together. The guillemot, however, is much more careless than its neighbour, and deposits its egg on the very edge of the cliff. There is no attempt at a nest: the egg is just laid on the bare rock. The eggs are large, and you rarely find two alike. The shape resembles that of a pear, so that, when the bird rises off the egg, it often spins around on its axis instead of falling over. Great numbers of eggs, however, do fall over the cliff edge.

Incubation, which is carried on by both birds, usually lasts about five weeks. When the young are hatched they are covered with a soft greyish-black down. They remain in the nest for about three weeks, and at the end of that period the back and breast are covered with short feathers, also the wings, caused by the rapid growth of the primary wing coverts. They are generally found on the sea about that period, but how they get down from the high cliffs is not quite known. It has been asserted by some naturalists that they are carried on the back of one of the parent birds, and by others that they are taken down with a hold of the wing—but this is doubtful. When they are about two months old the flight feathers proper begin to grow, and they are taught the art of diving, though they are rather reluctant at first. Except probably in the size of the bill the young birds, after the first month, are much about the same size as their parents.

During most of the year the guillemots and razor-bills live far out at sea, only coming in for a short period during the nesting season. They are excellent swimmers and divers, but the guillemot always seems to be a very stupid bird. It will float on the water until you are quite close to it, then suddenly it seems to discover that danger is near and down it goes.

You wait patiently for its return, watching all around for what seems a very long time, then it rises a considerable distance away, and sits and looks at you with the same stupid expression. It may be that it is conscious of its diving powers and wants to show off.

The razorbill is probably the more interesting bird of the two from the fact that, as it sits on the rock, it is the nearest approach in appearance of any bird—excepting perhaps the little auk—to the now extinct great auk. The St. Kildans say that the great auk was at one time on the island, though none of them can remember having seen one.

The black guillemot is also found on St. Kilda. It is a smaller bird than the common guillemot, and the whole of the plumage is black with the exception of a patch of white on the coverts of each wing. The webs, toes and legs are in striking contrast, being a bright vermilion, while the bill and claws are black. Like the common guillemot it makes no nest, but in comparison it seeks a place of great security to deposit its eggs. These are generally found in a deep crevice of the rock or amongst large stones on the beach. The clutch consists of two and they are of a great variety of colours, some white with greenish tinge, some blue, and others buff, all more or less blotched with brown.

Black guillemots are never found in large colonies, though several pairs may be found breeding near each other. Both sexes take part in incubation, and the young rarely leave their nest until they are fully feathered. The winter plumage is the exact antithesis of the summer dress. The crown is dark, and the back is barred with blackish brown and white,

K

while the wing primaries are black and all the rest white.

In the cormorant we have quite another order of bird, in which not only the feet but the hind toes are webbed. It has rather a sinister look as it sits perched on a shelving piece of rock, and Milton has compared this bird to his Satanic Majesty. The bill is long and straight except at the point, which is hooked and of a pale brown colour. The head and neck are black intermixed with a number of small, white, hair-like feathers. The back and wing coverts are a very dark brown, while the wings and tail are quite black. The breast and under parts are bluish black with two white patches on the thighs. The feathers on the top of the head can be elongated into a crest at will.

It builds on rocky ledges and sometimes on trees. The nest, which is large and high, is added to every year and sometimes reaches a height of four feet. It consists of an accumulation of grass, sticks or seaweed according to its location. It can easily be seen at a distance owing to its height, and the long outstretched neck of the bird sitting on it. The young are blind when hatched and are covered with long black down. The odour of decaying fish, etc. from a colony of cormorants is very offensive. The eggs, usually three in number, though sometimes four or five, are of a greenish colour and thickly encrusted with lime.

The cormorant lives entirely on fish and consequently is a diver. It sits with its head below the water, and whenever it sees a fish, down it goes with its wings closed without ever causing a ripple. When the fish is secured it is swallowed head first. This bird was protected at one time and there was a royal post of " Master of the Cormorants." The birds were trained to catch fish and come back to their master with them.   A brass ring was placed round the neck at its base to prevent the bird from swallowing the fish, and on its return its owner simply pulled the fish up its throat and the bird was liberated again. The practice is still continued in China.

One would almost imagine that cormorants had not been intended for diving birds, as their feathers are very easily saturated with water, and, after they have been immersed several times, they can be seen in great numbers sitting on the rocks with outstretched wings sunning themselves and drying their feathers. Their flight is very like that of a duck and they might easily be mistaken in the distance, as they fly just above the water with outstretched neck.

Doubtless many are aware of the fact that St. Kilda has a wren all its own, and it is the only land bird that need be mentioned, as everyone is fairly familiar with the others—the raven, hooded crow, starling, wheat-ear, etc.   I have seen the wren often, and had ample time to watch it, as it did not seem in the least afraid. I was slowly wandering amongst the rocks that line the bay one morning when I was attracted by a harsh chirp, and up jumped the little brown bird. I was more than agreeably surprised, for I had not expected to see it there.   It looks at first sight just like its mainland representative, and probably had I not known that it was a quarter of an inch longer I might not have noticed the difference, for it is very slight.   Its back, legs and toes are both stronger and lighter in the colour, and the markings are generally lighter and more defined than in our own bird. They are often found hopping about the cottages, and at the cleits. They seem to be fond of the rocks but prefer a hole in the cleits for building purposes. The nest is larger and not so neatly built as our own wren's. The eggs are also much larger and slightly mottled with brown ; in fact, the difference is more marked in the eggs than in the bird. There is a danger of the wren being exterminated, for its eggs are in great demand by collectors, and the natives are being constantly tempted to sell.

ST. KILDA.

The Village, looking east.

CHAPTER XV.

ST. KILDA—THE EVACUATION OF THE ISLAND.

" Farewell at last, brave Sentinel, to thee,
Lone outpost in a wild relentless sea."

SINCE the preceding chapters on St. Kilda were written events have moved rapidly there, and the St. Kildans all unconsciously have been making history; and people have been talking glibly about the lonely isle who had never heard of it before, or to whom at most it was only a name. During the long period in which it has been inhabited, the island has passed through many phases, but on Friday, the 29th day of August, 1930, the curtain was rung down on the last scene.

As if repenting for past misdeeds the angry Atlantic had ceased to lash the rocks with its wonted fury, and had crooned a lullaby all night long to the sleepless islanders. As the first streaks of dawn were colouring the eastern sky the St. Kildans were astir. And no wonder! For they were about to take the greatest risk they had ever taken—to say farewell to their island home which they all cherished so dearly. It was a sad silent band that trudged down the weed-grown path to the beach, past the church and manse to the jetty, where the crew of the Admiralty sloop, in their smart white duck uniforms, were waiting to receive them. Scarcely a ripple stirred the bosom of the water as the St. Kildans were taken out in launches to the *Harebell* lying in the bay, and with sad faces and tear-dimmed eyes took a last look at their beloved isle, as the boat steamed slowly away to " the land of promise," where the green hills of Morven look over the Sound to the dark blue peaks of Mull. The last page of the saga of St. Kilda was written, and the book closed, never to be opened again.

It would be interesting to know what the great black-backed gulls, sitting on the cliffs of Lavenish, thought when the *Harebell* steamed past with the faithful remnant of a brave people who had at all times succoured each other, and who had so courageously held on to their rock through storm and sunshine, peril, trial and hunger.

For a number of years the St. Kildans had to undergo great privations during the winter months, and were often hard-pressed for the necessaries of life before a boat could reach them in the spring with a supply of provisions. They were no grousers and knew what privation was, so that things must have been bad, in more ways than one, before they resolved to apply to the Government to be removed.

They had been threatened with epidemics and starvation before, and always came out of their ordeal with smiling faces and glad hearts. It was no new thing for them to fight the elements of Nature, and there was something more at the back of their minds than this. The population of the island, especially on the male side, had gradually declined, and though the women were willing workers, they had to depend upon the men for their existence. This may have been a strong factor in inducing the people to apply to the Government for help.

The removal of the St. Kildans to the mainland is no new suggestion, but few people ever dreamed that they would really leave the rock on which they had been cradled. As far back as 1877 the subject was hotly debated in the Scottish press, and Mr Seaton, in his book *St. Kilda, Past and Present*, published in the end of that year, devoted a whole chapter to it. He wrote that the discussion resolved itself into three suggestions : (1) To take the people off the island altogether ; (2) to leave them on the island under better conditions ; and (3) to remove them to the mainland during the winter months and return them to the island in the spring. All these proposals, however, ended in smoke, and the St. Kildans went on the even tenor of their way unconscious of having been in the fierce glare of the limelight.

There were many sad hearts on St. Kilda when the time of their departure drew near, for they had all been born and brought up on the lonely isle, and when the subject of leaving it was discussed in their parliament some years ago, one of the old women declared that the island would have to be bombarded before she would leave it.

Curiously enough, the latter condition was fulfilled, for on a smiling Monday morning in May, 1918, a German submarine rose just off the point of the Dun. The St. Kildans, thinking it a British boat, did not worry, and when it came on a level with the wireless station the shelling began. It was a terrible day on St. Kilda, and never before had there been such fear and excitement on the island. The people took to the hills as fast as they could run, and men, women and children were flying in all directions seeking a place of shelter. Happily no one was killed. The Germans fired seventy-two shells, and beginning with the old storehouse beyond the manse they partially levelled the village. The manse escaped, although the windows were shattered, but the church was completely demolished. The nurse's house and the wireless room received particular attention, but, strange to say, the masts were left. Apparently the visitors were suspicious about the use of the " cleits" on the slopes of Conachair, for they wasted several shells on them.

There is not much fear that the youth of the island will regret too deeply leaving their old home. Some have already left and made good elsewhere. But it is the old people who will feel the change of environment. Had they all been located together they might not have felt it so keenly ; they were a communal people, and separation to them must have been terrible. Some are gone to Ardness, Larachbeg, Achabeg, Savary and Lochaline ; and to far Strome Ferry the Fergusons and Finlay M'Queen, the once famous cragsman, whose iron grip of the hand I well remember.

Only those who know the western islands can appreciate the many hardships and difficulties the people have to contend with, and the inaccessibility of St. Kilda aggravated these trials in a marked degree. A number of years ago they were presented by the *Daily Mirror* with a wireless station, but were only allowed to use it for S.O.S. messages. Their extreme remoteness taught them the lesson of self-reliance: they lived in a little kingdom of their own ; they had their own parliament and were " a law unto themselves."

What the future has in store for them remains to be seen, but one may doubt if their lot will be a happier one. They will certainly never forget Hirta, for they will leave behind, " each in his narrow cell," many who were near and dear to them. They will miss the wild scream of the sea birds, which was music to their ears. They will miss the roar of the Atlantic billows, booming and echoing amongst the rocks and caves. In spring they will miss the return of the birds to which they looked forward so eagerly. All their lives they lived in expectation; now that is gone. The old homes they knew so well are now deserted and will crumble into decay—a village of the dead. Their ghosts will haunt the slopes of Oiseval, Conachair and Mullach Mor. They may not be there in the flesh, but they will be there in the spirit, for each and all of them, despite their hardships, loved the lonely isle, and its memory will linger with them at all times like a sweet melody.

CHAPTER XVI.

IONA TO-DAY.

" Far the cloudless sky stretches blue
        Across the isle
        Green in the sunlight."

AS you run up the Sound of Iona and drop anchor opposite the jetty, the little village lies before you, just a handful of houses scattered along the foreground of rocks, and flanked with a range of hills running north and south.

Close behind the village are the relics of the past—the ruins of the Nunnery, St. Oran's Chapel, the Crosses, and, farther north, the fine old Cathedral and Monastery ruins. Now there are many fine old ruins in other parts of Scotland which are much more easy of access, and one wonders what it is that attracts so many people to this far-away isle, for thousands of tourists from all parts of the world congregate in Oban every summer, and make the pilgrimage to Iona. It may be that the fame of St. Columba, the story of his struggles to uphold and further our Christian religion, has reached all parts of the world and causes a glamour to hang over this little isle. It may be to many merely a rarity or an interesting spectacle—it would be difficult to say. But once you have gone in the true spirit and lived on the island, there is an indescribable " something " which grips you, and holds you tightly in its grasp.

True, if you are an archaeologist, or an artist, or a

student of our Christian faith, there is endless work for you to do. If you are jaded and in want of peace and rest from the turmoil of life, or from the incessant tooting and blaring of motor horns, and all the nerve-racking noises of a busy city—then go to Iona, where you will find peace of soul and rest of mind.

There are always numbers of interesting people to be met on the island, either staying at one or other of the two small hotels or in one of the few houses or cottages which may be rented for the season. Mostly, they foregather at the post office to fetch the letters when they arrive by the Oban steamer. Authors and lecturers are to be seen—some of whom may have written books on the island. There are also artists in plenty who are busy transferring to canvas the great riot of colours that are constantly flitting over the sky and the waters of the Sound. Others are men and women content to see and learn and listen—and listening is a fine art which, alas, few nowadays cultivate !

There is only one road running from north to south through the northern part of the island. It branches in two at the village—the one fork going by the shore to Sligineach, while the other holds inland till it reaches the Machair, where it vanishes among sand and grass.

One of the great charms of the place is that you are free from restraint of any kind, and can wander whither your fancy leads without constantly being reminded that " trespassers will be prosecuted." The natives are kindness itself, and instead of turning you off their land will meet you with a friendly greeting. The very animals instead of running from you will come to be patted ; and even the dogs, who usually confront a stranger in outlying parts with anything but a friendly eye, will not only greet you there, but will follow you for a long distance from their home, frisking and dancing around with evident enjoyment.

I once asked a crofter how he accounted for this friendly spirit displayed by all the animals on the island, and his explanation was quick and to the point. " We never ill-treat our animals in any way," he said, " but always show them kindness. We rarely drive our sheep, but just lead the way, and they follow." This kindness is one of the striking characteristics of the natives of Iona and is doubtless a relic of the teaching of Columba, handed down through the long ages which have passed since that wonderful man lived in his wattle and daub hut by the lonesome sea shore.

Golfers may be delighted to hear that there is quite a good and sporting course on the island, with long stretches of beautiful turf interspersed with natural sandy bunkers and heath covered hillocks.

For bathers the island is a very paradise. Some parts of the shore are finely sheltered and there are long reaches of dazzling white sand, where not only sea-bathing but sun-bathing is greatly indulged in. Away at the north end, where the Danes landed and where they killed the Abbot and a number of monks, is to be found an enormous tract of sand—white as the driven snow, and still known as " The white strand of the monks." Again this white sand is to be seen down by the Machair, and on the east coast south of Sligineach, and the water looks so cool and green and tempting there that it has become for many the favourite bathing place of Iona.

Some beautiful Celtic work comes from the

IONA.

" Where you will find peace of soul and rest of mind."

island, executed in oxidized silver and enamel. The articles are designed by Mr and Mrs Alec. Ritchie. The work is delicate and beautiful, and the Celtic designs, copied from old crosses and tombs, are most intricate. Mr Ritchie is a keen archaeologist. He is the local custodian of the ruins, a great authority on everything Celtic, and a master of the Gaelic language.

Iona is quite a small island, about three and a half miles long and a mile and a half broad. To the uninitiated this may sound ridiculously small. But it takes some time to walk those three and a half miles —for what is not moorland is bog, what is not bog is great deep sandy bunkers, what is not bunker is heath-covered rock, what is not heath-covered rock is some mighty precipice grey with lichens and age, what is not precipice is deep valley, and what is not valley is some indentation of the sea bitten deep into the interior.

Every year the island is becoming more and more a haunt of artists—and no wonder, considering the great riot of colours to be found there at sunset, and the wonderful cloud effects that are seen towards evening. The waters opposite Eilean-nam-Ban too are ever changing ; sometimes they are a pale emerald or olivine, sometimes a deep azure, sometimes ultramarine. At times the whole aspect of the lands-cape will change with vivid suddenness. The ruins of the Nunnery and the Cathedral will lose their grey, time-worn look and assume hues of shell pink: such is the kaleidoscope of colour that is eternally painting anew these relics of the past. Then there are wonderful misty shades to be found in the interior of the old Cathedral—shades that are also ever changing as the restless sun moves round in space and streams in through the fine old windows, some of them crumbling in decay, and throws a dim religious light on all around.

In a little sheltered cove on the east coast is Martyrs' Bay, where the remains of the kings and chiefs were landed on their way to their last resting-place in the sacred soil of the Reilig Oran. The Road of the Dead led north from there, but has now entirely disappeared. It was a broad paved way and ran along by the Nunnery grounds, past the west side of the Maclean Cross and on to what was probably a burial place in the days of St. Columba.

The Nunnery had no connection with the saint: nunneries played no part in Columba's system. It was founded somewhere in the twelfth or the beginning of the thirteenth century by Reginald, Lord of the Isles, whose sister was the first Prioress. In the west gable of the chapel is a beautiful rounded window of thirteenth century design in perfect preservation and a consecration mark can be seen on the exterior of the gable.

The present road at this point runs almost parallel with what once was the Road of the Dead. Just at the bend where the beautiful Maclean Cross now stands, tradition says is the spot where St. Columba rested on his last walk, before death overtook him. The Maclean Cross is a tall, slender monolith formed out of a slab of mica schist, and stands about ten and a half feet high. It still shows some beautiful delicate tracery and scroll work, and the design is somewhat different from that found on the other crosses. It is said to date between the twelfth and thirteenth centuries.

Out of the many crosses at one time on the island the only complete ones remaining are the Maclean, St. Martin's, and the recently reconstructed St. John's. These crosses do not mark a grave or burial mound, but were erected for sweet remembrance sake.

A grassy patch enclosed by four walls is the little God's Acre of this isle—the Reilig Oran. Within it stands St. Oran's Chapel, and there are also Ridges of the Kings and of the Chiefs, where are gathered together for their preservation the tombstones and fragments that were scattered about. St. Oran's Chapel was built somewhere about the year 1093 and stands on the site of what apparently once was a chapel which may have been there in the days of St. Columba.

The King of the Picts and Scots was buried in the Reilig Oran about the year 860, and for centuries afterwards many of the other kings were brought there for interment, including Duncan and Macbeth. There also lie many Highland chiefs, commemorated by elaborately carved slabs of peculiar design, the workmanship of which, for the period, is unsurpassed.

I have often wandered to this sacred place to commune with Nature. Sometimes at nightfall, when all was silent, one would step gently on the soft turf so as not to disturb the sleepers, up between the Ridges of the Kings and the Chiefs, and on to the ruined chapel, and passing through the Romanesque doorway would lean on the arch, below which tradition says that St. Oran is peacefully waiting—waiting for the call. Ah! what peace of soul is there—nothing to disturb the silent sleepers save the soft murmur of the rippling waves lapping the near-by shore. Surely this is the most hallowed spot in all Scotland!

A stone's throw from the Reilig Oran stands the beautiful Cathedral, which has now been partly restored. It consists of a nave, transept and choir, also an aisle and sacristy. The doorway leading to the sacristy at once attracts attention for its marvellous beauty of design, and the arches of the choir are also worthy of note.

St. Martin's Cross stands in front of the main doorway of the Cathedral, and is well preserved. It is beautifully ornamented in front with a succession of large and small bosses interlaced with scrollwork, while the central panel on the reverse side consists of a representation of the Virgin and Child Christ surrounded by angels. From its style and design it is thought by experts to have been executed somewhere about the ninth or early tenth century. Professor Macalister in 1927 discovered a short inscription at the bottom of the Cross. He had the lichens which had grown over it carefully removed, and found that, in the manner of the age, it was a plea for a prayer for the man who had carved it.

St. John's Cross also stands in front of the Cathedral, just a little to the north of St. Martin's Cross. The ravages of time have told their tale on this cross, but Professor Macalister has been at work on it, along with his experts, and it has been restored as nearly as possible to its original design. Parts of the cross were discovered at different places on the island, and these have been pieced together in a

THE NUNNERY GROUNDS, IONA.

marvellous manner, and you can now see the cross almost as it originally stood. Dr. Joseph Anderson says that "This Cross is decorated in the purest style of Celtic art," and that "no finer specimen of art workmanship exists in Scotland." It is thought to be of an earlier date than St. Martin's Cross, and is probably the oldest on the island.

The Torr Abb, or Abbot's Hill, is also in front of the Cathedral, and some hold this to be the knoll that Columba ascended just before he died, but it was probably one farther to the north.

One could spend weeks wandering about amongst these wonderful relics of bygone days, on every stone of which history is written large if we could only read it. Much has already been discovered, but there are still a great many more discoveries of enthralling interest awaiting the archaeologist and the historian. The appeal of Iona is infinite, and will last for ever.

CHAPTER XVII.

COLUMBA OF THE WESTERN ISLES.

"He was a man of venerable life and blessed memory."—Life of St. Columba, by S. Adamnan.

COLUMBA, or to use his Irish name, Colum, had a tall and commanding figure, was possessed of good looks, and had a powerful, but sweet voice. He was born on Thursday, the 7th December, 521, in a small Irish village called Gartan, amongst the wilds of the Donegal mountains. His father and mother traced their descent from a line of kings of Ireland. Columba himself might have been a king, but he renounced all honours to become a soldier of Christ.

He went for his early training to Moville and Clonard, and before he left Clonard Monastery he was ordained a priest. When he left Moville he studied under an old Irish bard, and it was at this early age that he first acquired his great love for poetry, which he retained all through life. His first church was built on a hill, not very far from where he was born. There was an old round tower on the spot, one of the many to be seen in Ireland. The locality is still known as Long Tower. The church was erected in 545, when Columba was only twenty-four years of age.

During the next seventeen years he wandered up and down Ireland founding a great many churches or monastic buildings. He was a past master at organization and remained so all his days, and the experience he gained during his wanderings in Ireland was of great value to him in after life. It was when he established the monastery at Kells that his wonderful manuscript, the " Book of Kells," was produced. It is said to be one of the most beautiful and marvellous pieces of work in existence, the writing and lettering being perfect, and some of it almost microscopic.

He was an ardent student and read deeply in all the religious literature that came in his way, and during a visit to Clonard he saw in the church a beautiful copy of the Psalter belonging to St. Finnian. He immediately set about making a copy of it in secret, a work which cost him many a sleepless night. This book is sometimes referred to as " The Evangalorum " or Gospel Book, and sometimes as " The Psalter." St. Finnian discovered that Columba had copied the book and disputed his right to do so. He made an appeal to the High King of Ireland who gave judgment against Columba. The latter refused to give up his copy, and consequently was imprisoned but eventually made his escape.

In those days clan feeling ran high in Ireland, and Columba's kinsmen, thinking that the clan had been insulted, immediately offered battle at Culdreimhne. King Diarmait was defeated, and there was great slaughter on both sides. Although Columba won the fight, that seemed to offer him little or no consolation, and after some time, full of remorse and grief at the loss of so many gallant clansmen, he determined to leave Ireland and go on a pilgrimage to Alban.

This is the old Irish tale that has been handed down, but, curiously enough, Adamnan, Columba's biographer, makes no mention of it, but simply says that, "in the forty-second year of his age, wishing to make a pilgrimage for Christ from Ireland to Britain, he sailed forth." Along with twelve apostles Columba left the shores of Erin in a coracle, and landed on Iona in May, 563, in a rocky bay on the south side of the island known as Port-a-Churaich, which means "The Bay of the Coracle," now generally known as St. Columba's Bay. When Columba banished himself from Ireland he resolved that he would never again stay where he could see his native shores. A story is current amongst the isles that he first landed on Oronsay, but finding that he could still descry the distant shores of Erin he immediately put out again and sailed north until he landed on Iona.

His first act on landing was to turn up the valley to the left and climb the hill known as Carn-cul-ri-Eirinn, a rugged eminence of bare rock and heather, the highest point of which is now marked by a cairn. From there he could get an uninterrupted view across the sea towards the land whence he had come—but there was no land in sight in that direction, nothing but a wide expanse of rolling sea and foam-crested breakers. Here he was at last safe from the temptation to return and so he peacefully settled on Iona. For thirty-four years this little island was his headquarters—the centre from which all things of a spiritual nature radiated throughout the north.

He died on 27th June, 596, at the age of seventy-four, and was buried on Iona. A story is, however, current that in later years, during the ravages of the Norsemen, the sacred bones were transferred to Kells in Ireland for safety and were there buried beside those of St. Patrick.

PORT-A-CHURAICH.

*" A little rocky bay which was once nameless, but which is now known
as St. Columba's Bay."*

Like the glorious colours that paint its bold and rocky coast at sunset, the undying light of Christianity lingered in Iona when it had faded away in other lands, and bold God-fearing men braced themselves to the ordeal before them, and went forth to rekindle the flame and scatter the seeds of religion anew. It certainly requires some effort to believe that this lonely isle should have been the chosen place where the ancient faith was to be purified and revived to blaze with renewed vigour, while all over the Continent religion was in a chaotic state, and superstitious idolatry was practised everywhere.

The ordinary individual may be familiar with all that is known about Columba, and yet may never come to a true understanding of the real man. It requires the Celtic temperament to do this. He was a defiant leader in war, bold and courageous, yet he had the tender heart of a child, and the sweet simplicity of his great Teacher and Master, Christ. Here is a beautiful description of him by Fiona Macleod :—

" Columba was at once a saint, a warrior, a soldier of Christ, a great abbot, a dauntless explorer, and militant Prince of the Church : and a student, a man of great learning, a poet, an artist, a visionary, an architect, administrator, lawmaker, judge, arbiter. As a youth this Prince, for he was of royal blood, was so beautiful that he was likened to an angel. In mature manhood there was none to equal him in stature, manly beauty, strength, and with a voice so deep and powerful that it was like a bell, and once indeed, at the Court of King Bruidh, literally overbore and drowned a concerted chorus of sullen Druids. These had tried to outvoice him and his monks, little knowing what a mighty force the 64th Psalm could be in the throat of this terrible Culdee."*

*Iona by Fiona Macleod.

He had the roaming nature of his race, and even after he settled in that haven of havens, Iona, the old restless spirit would seize him, and he would become a wanderer again, but always in the furtherance of a religious cause.

In one of his restless fits he journeyed into the Pictish domain of Tiree and set up a sanctuary there. Fear of the sullen Pictish clans of his day did not deter him from journeying to their islands and setting up sanctuaries of rest and prayer. In those days the belief in spirits almost amounted to a religion in Alban. Spirits lurked everywhere—in the hills, the woods, the waters, and the air, and the Druids professed to be able to command these spirits. Columba resolutely set himself to destroy this belief and in its place set up true religion. With this object in view, he went to the mainland, accompanied by St. Comgall and St. Canice, and after terrible hardships reached the wilds of Perthshire and there founded a monastery. Thence he went to Inverness to face the King of the Picts and his all-powerful Druids, and by his resourceful nature and powerful persuasion the Cross succeeded where the sword had failed.

There are no authentic records of how he undertook these awful journeys through a land which was then roadless. Those who are familiar with this region of mountains, moors and bogs to-day will at once realize what a journey through these wilds must have meant in the sixth century, when there were only badly defined tracks through the bleak mountain passes. His route to King Brude's fort presumably lay through the great glen of Alban, now traversed by the Caledonian Canal.

There is one thing about Columba which must have stood out pre-eminently and worked strongly on the mind of the Gael. He was a patriot in every sense of the word, and loved his country; he was intensely proud of his race; he loved his clan; he was a true and staunch friend: all these qualities were indelibly marked in him. But what must have appealed most was that he was also possessed of the wonderful gift of religious foresight—better known perhaps as the "second sight," and this must have had a powerful effect upon a Gaelic people.

Some have averred that he was the first to possess this strange natural gift, but many authorities who are familiar with the ancient Gaelic literature doubt this, and hold that there are records of this second sight before Columba's time. Here is an illustration of his wonderful power in this respect. When he was living on Iona, St. Brendan died in Ireland, and the night following his death Columba suddenly alarmed his monks by calling upon them for a celebration of the Eucharist, as it had just been revealed to him that St. Brendan had been called by his Heavenly Father, and had died the night before. He said " Angels came to meet his soul, I saw the whole earth illumined with their glory."

Adamnan tells us that about a week before his death Columba knew full well that his days were numbered, and requested that he might be placed upon a waggon and taken over to the west side of the island (probably to the Machair) where his monks were busy with their respective duties on the land, so that he might speak with the brethren. He informed them that he had desired the Lord to spare

him a little longer so as not to turn their Easter
joy into sadness. Looking eastward he blessed
the island and its inhabitants and was then taken
back to the monastery.

A few days later, when Mass was being celebrated,
his countenance seemed to light up with joy and he
explained that he had seen the vision of an angel
hovering over him.

On the following Saturday, accompanied by his
faithful servant, Diormit, he went to bless the grain
stored in the granary. Having done so he informed
Diormit that that day would be truly a day of rest for
him, for at midnight he would depart to his Heavenly
Father. After this he left the granary and while
walking slowly towards the monastery he had to rest
by the way, and the place was afterwards marked by a
cross. While he was sitting there his faithful white
horse came to him and laid its head upon his breast.
The attendant was about to drive the horse away
when Columba said, " Let him alone, for he loves me."

He rose and climbed a little grassy knoll which
commanded a view of the monastery buildings and
stood there for some time looking around him, then
raising his hands to heaven he said :—

> " Upon this place, small though it be, and mean, not only
> the Kings of the Scotic people, with their peoples, but also
> the rulers of barbarous and foreign races, with the people
> subject to them, shall confer great and no common honour :
> by the saints also even of other churches shall no common
> reverence be accorded to it."

The little settlement founded by the Saint and
probably built of wood and wattle and daub—that is,

ST. COLUMBA'S PILLOW, IONA.

"*The bare rock for pallet and a stone for pillow.*"—*Adamnan's*
"*Life of St. Columba.*"

Photo by Winifred Wilson.

CLAMSHELL CAVE, STAFFA.

" *Surely it is the last word in peculiar rock formation.*"

branches of trees plastered together with mud—is presumed to have been somewhere near to the site of the present Cathedral, but no trace of it now exists. There is considerable diversity of opinion as to the exact site, and though Adamnan refers to the settlement several times in his life of Columba, his description is so vague that it is impossible to form any definite opinion. There is little doubt, however, that it was not on the site of the ruins of the later monastery, but farther north beyond the mill lade—probably somewhere near to Clachanach, or a little east from that ; in that case one of the little hillocks near Clachanach is likely to have been the knoll from which he blessed the island.

He then slowly descended and walked to his hut where he sat down and once more continued the transcription of his Psalter. His strength seemed to fail, however, when he reached the middle of the 33rd Psalm, for he stopped at the foot of the page of his manuscript and wrote no more.

He was able to attend Vespers and then returned to his hut again. With his life slowly ebbing away he lay down on the uneven rock which was his bed. A large round stone incised with a rough cross did duty for a pillow. (This stone is preserved in the Cathedral to this day). Lying there he gave his last commands to his monks and then seemed to lapse into rest.

When the midnight bell pealed out he immediately rose and obeyed its call for the last time. He was the first to reach the church and immediately sank on his knees before the altar. Diormit followed him, and finding his master lying there he gently raised his head, and laid it on his breast. The monks arrived with lights and found him dying. He was scarcely able to speak, but with the assistance of Diormit he raised his right hand and blessed them just as the spirit was leaving the earthly tabernacle and taking its flight to the realms he had so often spoken of.

Thus ended the life of a great and wonderful man—a born leader and commander, a scholar, a poet, a seer, and a militant soldier of Christ.

The benign beauty and simplicity of his life are still reflected down through the long centuries that have passed, and have left their traces on the natives to this day.

The island before he came was simply known by the Gaelic name of Hy or I, meaning The Island, but afterwards it was known as " I Chaluim Chille "—the Island of Columba of the Church.

The story of his life reads almost like a tale of romance. Truly it can be said of him—*Veni, vidi, vici*—I came, I saw, I conquered. He crossed the raging seas in a fragile coracle, he gradually subdued the unruly Picts and captured the love of their king and overcame the influence of the once all-powerful Druids. He set up an independence which Scotland had never known before, and in his wake followed civilization and a better mode of life for the people.

And all this happened more than thirteen hundred years ago.

CHAPTER XVIII.

IONA AFTER COLUMBA.

" I-mo-Chree, my heart's own isle,
    Where monks intoned, now cattle low."

Macleod.

THERE can be little or no doubt but that the bright star in the firmament of the west gradually waned after the death of Columba. Iona enjoyed a certain spell of peace for years, and the Abbots and their monks went on the even tenor of their way, but the great influence of their wise and generous leader was missed and little or nothing is heard of any importance for the next two centuries. Iona was still the Iona of old. The beautiful blue waters of the Sound surged and rolled in their restlessness just as they had when the soldier of peace stood on the little hillock and blessed the island. The sun was still rising over Mull and setting in its triumphant blaze of grandeur away behind the distant Hebridean hills. Boats came and went at intervals, some to pay their respects to the little community that had so bravely carried the flag of Christ through many a storm and whose fame had reached to distant lands and kindled anew the torch of truth and salvation. Some came in dismal funeral array seeking the peace of the Sacred Isle, where they might commit their loved ones to the care of the wind-swept Reilig Oran.

But a day came when the sea brought a fleet over its waterway, and the Sound swarmed with galleys, not manned by men of peace but by bringers of death and destruction. The first arrival of these Scandinavian pirates occurred exactly two hundred years after Columba's death. They swept the island in their savagery, leaving only fear and terror in their wake. Four years later they returned, and this time they fired the monastery and left nothing but a mass of smoking ruins behind them. But worse was to follow, for in 806 they were again sighted in the Minch, and sixty-eight monks went bravely down to the beach to defend their island home. The pirates in their great galleys drew into a little bay to the south of the village, and while the monks were making a gallant attempt to prevent their landing they were completely outnumbered and ruthlessly killed. The little creek is known to this day as Martyrs' Bay.

It was quite apparent at last that something would have to be done to stop this ruthless pillage and massacre, so in 814 the headquarters of the Primate was moved to Kells in Ireland, and there remained for a considerable time. The brethren of Iona, however, remained staunch to the island, where Columba centuries before had pointed the way. They rebuilt the monastery—this time of stone, on a site adjoining the present Cathedral. A number of years later, however, it was again attacked by the Norsemen, and many of the brethren were killed while at worship.

Adamnan, the biographer of St. Columba, was abbot from 679-704, and created some little stir amongst the brethren by trying to introduce into the Celtic Church the Roman usage in connection with the date of Easter. Adamnan visited Ireland in

THE BENDING PILLARS, STAFFA.

"Suggesting to the mind that they had not been able to support
the enormous weight above them."

692 and again in 697 on matters relating to the church, and it was some time during that interval that he is supposed to have written his wonderful life of Columba. It is a brilliant piece of work, and if for nothing else his name will ever be remembered by students of Christian literature.

In 1093 the western isles fell into the possession of Norway. King Magnus being anxious to pay his respects to the sacred isle from which Columba's fame had spread, paid a friendly visit in 1097, but from this time onward for a long period of years there is a blank in the history of the island.

Towards the end of this period of silence (about the year 1140) we learn that the isles had been divided between Gadred of Norway and Somerled, the Celtic ruler. Meantime Somerled had married a Norwegian Princess, and their son, Reginald, had been made Lord of the Isles. Gadred objected to this, and a battle was fought to settle the dispute, but neither side could claim a decisive victory and the isles were divided between them, so Iona remained in the hands of a Celt.

Amongst the first things that Reginald did after he succeeded his father was to establish a monastery of Benedictine monks on Iona. He also created the order of Augustinian Canonesses of the Nunnery. There were but a few left of the old Columban Order of Monks, and these were promptly evicted by the new Benedictines, but a number of bishops and abbots and their followers came over from Ireland to avenge this insult, and after a struggle razed their building to the ground.

The reign of the old Columban Order, however,

was short-lived, for all that remained of the monks left the island in 1204, the Order having held sway for nearly six hundred and forty-one years. So the Benedictines were left in possession until the Reformation.

In 1693 the Duke of Argyll became owner of the island, and the eighth Duke handed over the ruins to the care of the Church of Scotland.

The chief character in the great drama of Iona was Columba, and so far as religion was concerned, the curtain practically fell with his death, when the fierce limelight which blazed on the island from 563 to 596 was extinguished.

A long period of turbulent centuries followed—and then there was a slumber. But an awakening came—the Church of Scotland took over the ruins, and the Cathedral has been restored. The Nunnery buildings are also receiving skilful attention to preserve them from falling into further decay, and the three crosses are being carefully watched and preserved ; and thus the peaceful to-day and the turbulent yesterday are now linked hand in hand in a joyous grasp.

I have given in Chapter XVI.—"Iona To-day"—some description of the ancient buildings and crosses because, although they properly belong to the centuries after Columba, they are an important and integral part of the Iona of to-day.

CHAPTER XIX.

STAFFA AND ITS CAVES OF MUSIC.

"Nature herself, it seemed, would raise
A minster in her Maker's praise."

Scott.

I SHALL never forget the first time I visited Staffa—one of the wonders of the world.

When we left Iona it was early morning, and the sun was shimmering through a filmy haze on a sea of oxidized silver. Thousands of little waves were catching up the faint rays and flashing forth their fairy lamps to greet the morn. There was practically no wind blowing in from the skerries that morning ; only a soft zephyr could be felt, and this was chiefly caused by the rate at which our little motor boat was travelling.

Coll and Tiree were long yellow sandhills lying away on our port side, like a mirage in the flickering heat haze all around. As we drew farther away from them they seemed to change in colour, and assumed a faint pink hue. Nearer lay the Treshnish Isles with the fantastic "Dutchman" always prominent, while away on the starboard side lay Gometra and Ulva, with the bluff cliffs of Mull standing out bold and threatening in the background.

Our motor hummed merrily as we sped over the waters, trailing our hands along the surface for a little diversion, or trying to catch the mimic lights flashing from our bows like sparks from a live electric wire. Quaint little puffins in search of a morning meal kept bobbing up and down in front of us, and would rise on the water and gaze in that odd inquisitive way the puffin has. They would then topple over and disappear, or flapping their little wings make off in great excitement, only to drop on the water again a little ahead. Cormorants were also on their favourite feeding ground, and being alarmed by the excitement of the puffins would make off in great haste; but being more wary birds would take care to keep well out of our reach. Razorbills and guillemots, both of an enquiring turn of mind, seemed to think us objects of curiosity, and we would be almost on them before they realized that they had better get down below to safer quarters.

A tiny speck, black as a piece of precious jet, lay far ahead and seemed to rise out of the rippling waters alive with sea sparkle. As we drew nearer it gradually assumed the proportions of a bold and rocky island, and I could discern through my binoculars the formation of the basaltic cliffs of Staffa. The island forms almost the centre of a group, and is eight miles north of Iona, while the nearest inhabited island is Gometra, about four miles distant. It is nearly three-quarters of a mile long, about a quarter of a mile broad, and its highest point, which is at the extreme southern end, is about one hundred and thirty feet above sea level. It is composed of a very dark, almost black, basaltic rock, which is as hard as flint, and gave out a sharp metallic ring when it came in contact with the steel clinkers in my hobnailed boots. It decomposes at parts, but the erosion is

GREAT COLONNADE, STAFFA.

"*At each step new wonders are revealed.*"

STAFFA.

Approaching the Cave of Music.

very slight, and goes no further; where it occurs the rock becomes slightly lighter in colour.

We were now nearing the island, and with the exception of a swell coming in from the Atlantic the sea was calm—too calm, for we might be disappointed in not hearing the music of the caves to perfection. Indeed, it was open to question whether the great natural organ would be playing at all, for on such a perfect day it seemed doubtful if the organist would not be too lazy even to run his fingers over the keyboard. However, after all we were not disappointed.

We ran our boat into a natural inlet on the east side of the island. This forms an excellent landing place, and is well sheltered, while the many broken pillars on the north side of the inlet make anchorage secure. There lay before us the wonderful Clamshell Cave. It cannot be called beautiful, but surely it is the last word in peculiar rock formation. This cave derives its name from its shape, which is like an enormous clamshell set on end. It is scooped out like a shell on one side, and the great pillars forming the inside are bent in a natural curve running down from top to bottom, then bending slightly downwards to the cave's mouth. The opposite side is quite different, being composed of many small broken pillars projecting from the face of the rock. As one stands on the edge of the little terrace adjoining the cave the effect is bewildering.

A scramble over the slippery rocks, and some climbing up the face of the pillars brings you to the narrow entrance of the causeway. Just opposite this point and separated by a channel some twelve or thirteen feet in breadth, is the Herdsman—a small conical

M

islet on the south. Through this channel the sea surges and rushes with great force. The beauty of the Herdsman is best seen from above, whence it resembles a huge honeycomb. On the one side it tapers gradually upwards, while the northern side consists of thousands of long slanting pillars running down from the apex to the sea.

As we proceed along the causeway examination reveals that it is composed of the irregular tops of basalt pillars, arranged more or less in long parallel terraces, the one below the other until they reach the sea. The tops of many of these pillars are flat, while others are concave, some very deeply concave, and numbers convex. These wonderful pillars are by no means the same, some having four and six sides, and some more, while one or two beyond the " Bending Pillars" are almost square. They vary in size, but the majority measure about two or three feet across.

Farther along the Causeway, which is of considerable length, you come to the " Bending Pillars." They are a row of columns, and the mass of solid rock above them, being about three times their height, suggests to the mind that they had not been able to support the enormous weight above them, and at some time had bent slightly inwards at the top.

As you stand here alone, and gaze on either side, the vastness and loneliness become overpowering. You feel at times afraid to move, for the noise of your steps on the hard basalt rock echoes along the terraced causeway and gives you the feeling that you are wandering amongst the ruins of a city of the dead—of some long-forgotten age. Though you are within sight of Gometra and Mull and Iona, a dread loneliness seems to lurk in every nook and cranny.

At each step new wonders are revealed and the grandeur of the whole structure is on such a vast scale that you cannot comprehend its meaning. When one attempts to describe it, words fail. No one has ever been able to speak of it so as to convey to the mind what one feels when wandering amongst its pillars and caves. Staffa stands as a wonderful example of Nature's craftmanship veiled in solitary grandeur, a lone isle guarded by the great Atlantic swell.

Its sides are pierced with many caves, but the most wonderful of all is the far-famed Fingal's Cave. As you approach it, a low eerie booming sound is distinctly heard, which increases in volume as you pick your way cautiously along. On rounding a slight curve you are confronted with the enormous mouth of a yawning cavern, and you find yourself gazing in awe and wonder into its black and fearsome depths. Why it is called Fingal's Cave seems to be a subject for controversy; I, however, prefer to call it by its euphonious Gaelic name, Uaimh Bhinn, the cave of music.

At low tide the tops of the broken pillars run a considerable distance out into the sea, and from this coign of vantage an excellent view of the exterior of the cave can be had, but it is wise to make sure that the tide is on the ebb, for it rushes in with great speed when it is on the flow. It occurred to me when sitting on the outmost pillar how inadequate any description of this wonderful cave would be. To appreciate its magnitude and its marvellous architectural beauty it must be seen. It looks as if it had been designed by some eminent architect skilled in that particular kind of work, and the whole structure carved, hewn and carried out under his close inspection and care.

Let us go into the cave. You can scramble along the right hand side for nearly two hundred feet, and then you are still some twenty or thirty feet from the end. It is over sixty feet high, and about fifty feet broad at the mouth, where the depth of water is over twenty feet. The roof is composed of the bottom of a mass of pillars which look as if they had been cut across. It is covered with lichens of various hues, some red, some deep orange, and some pale yellow, which gives a fresco effect to the otherwise dark surroundings. At times when the swell is heavy it breaks on the rocks and smothers up the mouth of the cave in a mass of spray. It is an awe-inspiring sight to stand at the extreme end in the semi-gloom, and look around. The columns arranged along each side are like the pipes of some mighty organ, and you seem to be in a lone cathedral aisle not made by hands. One feels almost bereft of speech, or at least inclined to talk only in whispers. But of what use is speech there? The incessant booming of the great Atlantic swell, as it surges up the narrow channel is like peals of muffled thunder which echo and reverberate until the whole cave seems to shake. Then weird musical notes creep into the confusion of sounds, as if unseen hands were running over the keyboard of this mighty organ, and one is reminded of the overture to the *Valkyrie* on a grand scale. It is marvellous, weird,

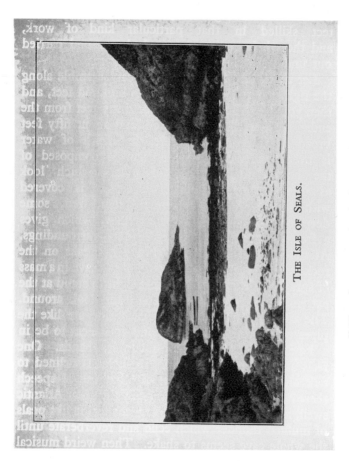

THE ISLE OF SEALS.

"*There is a rapture by the lonely shore*
There is society where none intrudes."

Photo by Winifred Wilson.

and uncanny.   One wonders what the effect would be like during a storm.   It would be a case of the wind, the waves, and the listener all going mad together.   It is cold, creepy and damp, and you feel that at any moment an array of formless spirits may step from the gloomy darkness at the back of the cave, and demand to know what your presence means in their holy of holies.   At times the eeriness has a fascinating effect and you can scarcely drag yourself away from its grip ; you feel that you are part of another world.   But the chill air warns you that you had better be gone, and it is comforting to stand again in the bright warm sunshine outside.

Fingal's Cave has been a theme for musicians and poets; the mad revel of wind and water, combined with the screaming of the sea birds and the black gloomy surroundings gave inspiration to Mendelssohn's mind, and the result was one of his finest overtures, which was named after the cave.

The causeway terminates at the mouth of the cave, and the other caves are best seen by boat.

The Great Colonnade which runs between Fingal's and Mackinnon's Caves is a long ridge of pillars about fifty feet high, packed closely together.   It gives a fine idea of the columnar structure of the island. The top is formed of a conglomerate mass of basalt with no regular formation.   It is covered at some parts with strong sea grass, but at others there is excellent pasturage for sheep.   Here and there, particularly towards the coast line, the tops of pillars protrude through the turf.   This is very pronounced above Fingal's Cave, where the grass is very scanty, and doubtless these are the pillars which form the roof of the cave.   While you stand there the tumultuous confusion of sounds going on below can be distinctly heard and resemble the muttering of a distant thunder storm.   If you care to risk yourself near enough to the edge of the cliffs at this point, a fine view can be had of the rows of columns at the beginning of the Great Colonnade.

There is no one living on Staffa, but there are some ruins of what once was a cottage near the centre of the island.   It was used by a shepherd, who refused to stay because of the loneliness of the place.   There is a small well near the ruins, but you have to search very carefully for it.   It lies about a hundred yards away near the top of the cliff.

The only signs of life are a few sheep peacefully grazing on the top, the cormorants in their own particular cave, and the puffins on the north-east side of the island.   With the exception of the distant roar of the Atlantic, silence reigns supreme up there.

To reach the top you have to travel a considerable distance around the coast line, or climb a long steep ladder running up the left side of the Clamshell Cave, and from there you have a pretty stiff climb to the cairn.   The island is divided by a narrow valley running from east to west, the northern part being much larger than the southern.   The ruins and the well are in the northern part.

The cairn at the highest point commands an extensive panorama of sea and islands, particularly towards the north and west.   The Treshnish Isles lie in a scattered mass almost at your feet, and just behind them the long low forms of Coll and Tiree seem as if lazily floating on the water.   Northwards,

Oreval, Haskeval and Halival, the sharp, jagged tooth-like peaks of Rum, stand boldly out in all their rugged glory. Farther north the Black Coolins cut the sky into a perfect fretwork pattern, and form a background of wild desolation, while at times fleeting vistas of the Outer Hebrides float across the vision away in the far north-west.

Before leaving the island I climbed up to the cairn to have a last look across the waters I had often seen stormy and frolicsome, and in their glee lashing with fury the barren rocks and skerries scattered all around, but that night they were placid and calm with a heat haze gradually spreading over all. The Treshnish Isles were faintly visible, while the sand dunes of Coll and Tiree were lost to sight. The sun was getting low in the western sky, and dimly shining through a veil of molten gold, so I retraced my steps reluctantly to my friend and his little motor boat which was lying at the mouth of the Clamshell Cave, and bade adieu to the caves of music.

CHAPTER XX.

IN THE SOUND OF IONA.

" So we will go a-sailing
Aroon, by the western isles."

Macleod.

THE ferry across the Sound to Fionnphort in Mull is just about a mile ; no great distance on a fine day, and you will find the ferryman very pleasant company. The Sound, however, is subject to the vagaries of the weather, and should it be in a frolicsome mood you will have a lively time before you reach Fionnphort. Coll, the old ferryman (now retired), had two boats—a motor boat and an ordinary row boat with a lug sail. While crossing one day when the weather was in a genial mood and the sea on its best behaviour, the conversation turned to which boat he preferred. He was cautious in giving a decided opinion, but at last admitted that he was not over-fond of the motor boat unless the Sound was calm, when he crossed in a shorter time, but when the sea was rough he much preferred his old row boat and lug sail. In winter time he used nothing else. For days on end during the stormy months he could not cross unless there was some very urgent case of illness, for there is no doctor on Iona. But should an emergency of this sort arise neither the ferryman nor the doctor is ever found wanting. Under such conditions he had crossed the ferry with

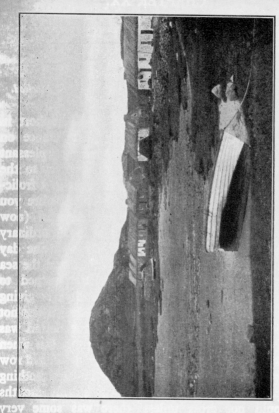

KINTRA, MULL.

"*The tiny thatched cottages have their peat stacks built up in front of the doors.*"

Photo by Winifred Wilson.

Landing Stores, Iona.

Excitement at the jetty. The "Dunara Castle" has arrived!

Photo by Winifred Wilson.

the doctor and been driven far out of his course, but always managed to land him on some part of the island. The life of the doctor and the ferryman is not always an enviable one and they require stout hearts to brave the elements at times. Coll is now enjoying a well earned rest, and a young man has taken his place.

I have never heard of any one attempting to swim the ferry but was told a remarkable story of the swimming powers and endurance of a cow and a dog in this respect. Both animals were taken over in the boat to Fionnphort one day and left there. The following morning their former owners on Iona were awakened by the barking of a dog, and on getting out of bed to see the cause of this early disturbance were astonished to find both cow and dog patiently waiting outside their old home. They had apparently been dissatisfied with their new quarters, and had taken to the water and crossed the Sound during the night. It would have been interesting to know whether they had crossed together.

The ferry is in great demand during the summer months, and would be more so if the route from Fionnphort to Salen or Craignure and the mainland were better known. The road is at present bad but the run is an alluring one through some of the wildest and grandest scenery in Mull. It is wild in the wildest sense, especially through Glen More, where the mountains rise on either side with a scowl and a threat on their dark scarred faces and seem intent on crushing you in their ponderous jaws. It is with a sigh of relief that you come to an open space, and feel you have escaped and can breathe freely again. It is about forty miles from Fionnphort to Craignure, and the driver has little respect for his engine or car, his main object being to get you to the pier in time for the boat. You are never certain when you start whether you will arrive there or not, but this glorious uncertainty is all a part of the day's play. If you don't it will be no fault of the driver, for with one sharp eye on the road in front, a merry twinkle in the other, a broad grin on his face, a mass of curly hair blowing in the breeze, and ever alert for trouble, he jolts you over hill and dale at a wonderful speed, and as he swings round some sharp corner or crashes through a heap of stones your dismay is allayed as he glances round with the same cheery smile. Such is the Mull motor man, and if this should reach his eye it is to be hoped he will recognize his picture and that the same devil-may-care look will spread over his handsome features.

But to return to the Sound.

It is extremely restful to sit on a calm summer evening and watch the palpitating bosom of the Sound rising and falling with a gentle swaying motion as it is affected by the swell of the Atlantic breakers far out at sea. The pleasure boats are busy on such a night and far into the darkness you can hear voices and the splash of the oars, or the beat of a motor engine, although you cannot see from whence the sound comes. Incidentally, many of these boats are painted a startling blue; indeed, that same blue seems to be very much used for all purposes by the natives of Iona. What their partiality is for such a strong colour would be difficult to say.

The picture is perfect when the moon rises over Erraid with its long, silvery sheen like the tail of a comet dancing and flickering on the calm placid waters.

There are nights, however, when you cannot sit on the open rocks and are glad of the shelter of a projecting ledge. At these times there is something sublime in the roar of the angry waves as they dash themselves in their fury against the island. Then comes a short lull, and the swish-swish of the returning wave as it rushes down the sandy beach, only to be thrown back again. It has a weird fascination, and you feel the power of Byron's words,

> " There is a rapture by the lonely shore,
> There is society where none intrudes
> By the deep sea and music in its roar."

There are a great many lovely islands dotted all round the coast of Iona ; the chief one in the Sound is Eilean-nam-Ban. It is said that Columba had all the women and cows banished to this island. It is to be hoped that the story is only traditional, for if it were true it would not redound to the fair name and fame of the Saint. Probably the story originated from the old couplet,

> " Far am bi bo bidh bean,
> S' far am bi bean bidh mallachadh."*

There is a lonely isle in the south end of the Sound which is a paradise of white heather and royal ferns. Here the *Osmunda Regalis* is more plentiful than our common ferns on the mainland. My friend, Captain Maclean, who owns a motor boat, offered to take me

*" Where there is a cow, there will be a woman,
Where there is a woman, there will be mischief."

out to explore it.   Think of what this meant to a lover
of ferns who thought that the " royal " was almost
extinct in Scotland!   Away we went one day and with
the motor running merrily were soon dancing over
the heaving waters of the Sound.   A fresh breeze
was blowing in from the Atlantic, and the waves were
tipped with foam, while every here and there " white
horses " were scurrying over the crest of the big
breakers.   After a considerable amount of heaving
and buffeting we slipped into a little bay on the lee
side of the island.   At first it looked as if no landing
could be made there, for the rocks rose sheer out of
the water, but after some manœuvring we managed
to jump on to a seaweed-covered ledge and scramble
up.   It was hard climbing for a minute or two until
we reached a gully where better foothold was to be had.
Making our way upwards over boulders and pinnacled
rocks, some covered with lichens and some with stunted
heather, at last we reached a plateau where we could
see around us.   Here we first sighted the white heather
which grows so plentifully on the island that in a few
minutes several bunches were picked.   I have lost
all faith, however, in the saying that it always brings
luck to those who find it.   Had I been content with a
single sprig the charm might perhaps have worked,
but being greedy probably I paid the penalty.

The white heather having lost its charm for the time
being, we set about exploring for the ferns, and in a
few minutes in a little boggy hollow the *Osmunda
Regalis* were discovered growing in tropical profusion.
They were so thick and entangled that one could
not walk through them—quite a jungle.   I envied
the proprietor of that little island of white heather and

DUN I, IONA.

" *Guardian of the Pool of Eternal Youth.*

royal ferns and wished that I could transport it to my garden, but my friend informed me that he would take me later to a spot on the island of Mull where the ferns were just as plentiful, and whence I could carry away as many specimens as I wished.

We got into the boat again after much scrambling over the steep and slippery rocks and set our course for Soa about three miles distant to the west. This island is still a great haunt of seals, as it was in the days of the monks, who used the island as a breeding station for keeping up the supply. They used the seals as food.

Soa looked at from some distance seems to be inhospitable and inaccessible, but in reality it is quite the reverse. It has a beautiful natural harbour running right up into the centre of the island, while another intersects it from the north-west. Its great charm is its high cliffs and perfect seclusion. You can lie there and watch the seals sprawling on a rock in the sunshine, and playing in the water, while every here and there a black head pops up and disappears again. There are also guillemots, razorbills and puffins on the rocks, while gannets occasionally sail overhead. Both the greater and lesser black-backed gulls are fairly plentiful amongst the islands, and on one of them the storm petrel builds.

The homeward journey was very enjoyable as the wind had fallen and we had the tide with us. We took the west side of Iona this time, hugging the shore nearly all the way. We gava Eilean Chalbha and its many projecting reefs a wide berth, and keeping north of Findlay's Rock held straight across the northern end of the Sound for Kintra on the Mull side, and its promised nursery of ferns.

The entrance to the natural harbour is bold and rocky and would have delighted the hearts of a band of merry smugglers. It is just the kind of place where a cargo of contraband could be safely landed on a starry night with a moonless sky. It runs a considerable distance inland, and the tiny thatched cottages are ranged in a straggling semi-circle round it. Each one has its peat heap stacked up in front of the door. The natives welcomed us warmly in Gaelic, but they also speak English with a charming accent. My friend talked with them in Gaelic and ultimately borrowed a spade from an old man with which to dig up the ferns.

Our route lay east through some low meadow land where the good folks were busy amongst their hay. With a friendly salutation we passed on and soon reached our destination, the Allt-na-Creiche, a slow, sedgy stream bordered on either side for some distance with a miniature forest of royal ferns. Here at last was the " royal " in its natural habitat with its fronds spread out in all their graceful beauty and the spore cases rising up like great clusters of bronze-coloured flowers.

Wading into the stream we soon dug up a number of roots. Suddenly there was a loud crack and the handle of the spade parted company with its old friend the blade, and so ended our expedition. We had got all the ferns we required, however, and marched solemnly back with our load and the broken spade to Kintra.

The old man's face fell several degrees when he

saw what had happened, but the smile came back again when we informed him that we would run into Fionnphort, where there is a dry goods store—one of those places where you can purchase anything from a needle to an anchor—and send him a new spade.

We were soon speeding down the Sound again, past Eilean-nam-Ban and into Fionnphort. Our mission being accomplished there, we started on our homeward journey across the ferry, and soon discovered that something unusual was going on. The *Dunara Castle* had arrived with stores and was lying at anchor in the Sound. She was taking on a cargo of sheep, which always causes great amusement to the onlookers as they have to be taken out to her in boats.

We arrived at the jetty safely after having spent nearly a round of the clock amongst the islands and on the heaving breast of the restless ocean. Our boat was gaily decorated with purple and white heather, and a small forest of royal ferns, while Prince, a little wire-haired terrier, stood guard at the bows.

We lost no time in dropping anchor and getting ashore and were soon tramping along the road to Sligineach, for we were as hungry as the proverbial hawk out on a hunting expedition.

CHAPTER XXI.

IONA, THE ISLE OF DREAMS.

*" True, I talk of dreams, which are the children of
an idle brain, begot of nothing but vain fantasy."*
                                        Romeo and Juliet.

IONA is so small compared with some of the
other Hebridean Isles that, speaking in metaphor, you could almost hold it in the palm of your
hand. It is bleak and barren in some parts, with
its bones protruding every here and there through a
coat of heather and coarse grass. Despite its small-
ness and bleakness this bare-ribbed island is distinctly attractive, alluring—and something more.

Its people are few, but they have a peculiar charm
of their own, and what they do and how they live
would be difficult to tell—but that is nobody's business.

There are many roads that lead to Iona, the
principal and easiest one being by the great waterway from Oban daily (excepting Sundays), and by
that road all sorts and conditions of people pour into
the island every summer. But they only remain for an
hour or so and then leave again for the more crowded
ways of life. Some of them are just the idle, curious
folk, and some are not, but in any case none of them
ever see or understand the island. They come and
go, and some wonder how any one can exist in such a
place ; but the *seekers* remain.

There is another road to Iona trodden only by the
few. It passes through the gates of dreamland to

The Machair Plain.

"Fairies still dance on their accustomed playground."

Photo by Winifred Wilson.

where the fairies gambol when night's candles are lit
in the deep blue dome of a Hebridean sky.   Once
upon a time I passed over that road.   The enchantment of the little Valhalla took possession of me, and
before I had reached the jetty the spell was cast and I
found myself a dreamer on the Isle of Dreams.   Little
wonder too, when once you have climbed to the top
of the hill behind the village when the sun is setting.
The great molten ball of fire is dipping on the horizon,
and splashing the sea with crimson and gold and
mauve and saffron; the rippling waves catch up the
glorious colours and scintillate and sparkle like living
fire or gems in a king's crown.   Then comes the
wonderful afterglow lighting up the waters all around
with diffused and softened light.   Many have tried
to paint this scene, but no artist's brush can ever do
justice to it.   A short twilight follows, then a pale
crescent moon rises slowly over the bluff cliffs of
Mull, casting its silvery sheen over the rippling waters
of the Sound.

Once you have seen this glorious picture you too
will become a dreamer on the Isle of Dreams.

In the long summer nights when there is no darkness and only a soft twilight falls, fairies still dance
on their accustomed playground on the Machair
plain.   The little knoll is called *Sithean Mor*, the
Fairies' Hill.   Columba's monks knew it as *Colliculus
Angelorum*.   It is a beautiful grassy hillock redolent
with the perfume of wild thyme and sweet-scented
herbs, charmingly painted with the pink and the blue
of the wild sea-thrift and delicate harebell, the same
knoll where St. Columba himself used to lie and
commune with the angels.   Some day you too may

N

lie there in the sweet-scented air, and hear the soft music of the lapping waves on the distant shore.   And you too may fall into a reverie and forget that there is such a thing as time—you too may become a dreamer on the Isle of Dreams.

Many are the queer happenings on this elfin isle.

In the dim shadows when the soft grey curtain of the night has fallen, a " something " lurks—you may call it fantasy, but it is not, and it is only given to the few to know of its existence.   Have you ever been out at the witching hour when the night is dark and the path is lonesome ?   Then you are often conscious of something beside you, near to you—it may be human or it may not, you cannot tell—but you know it is there, although you can neither see nor hear it. But its presence in some mysterious way is felt—and that is why I say a " something " lurks.

The Dream Isle has always been steeped in legend and story from long before the days when Colum came in his coracle, but to tell all these tales would take a book in itself, and you might not believe them if they were told, for they seem but the figment of dreams.

It chanced once that three pilgrims found themselves wandering on the high cliffs above the Machair, known as the Hill of Noises.   It is near to the same sands where Colum foretold that a crane would alight after its long flight from Ireland and ordered one of his monks to go there to succour the bird on its arrival.   The three were evidently in search of something which they could not find, and were sorely puzzled at their failure.   They had found it the day before and yet that day, try as they would,

they failed.   Everything seemed changed and different.
Strange though this may seem, it is true.   Tired
with their search they threw themselves down on the
springy heather which was plentiful up there.   They
lay there dreaming in silence until they saw a man
standing on a rock a few paces away, evidently watching them.   He left the rock and seemed as if making
towards them, but on looking a few seconds later they
found that he had completely vanished as if he had
never been.   They were mystified but said nothing,
and lay wondering what occult power was at work.
Their thoughts were disturbed by one of the three
suddenly rising and saying, " There is something
strange about this place.   I cannot understand it."
The others silently acquiesced; all three slowly wandered across the heather and down the cliff face
absorbed in their own thoughts, and dreaming their
day dreams of the enchantment of the cliffs.

On the north side of the Dream Isle is a lofty
eminence known as Dun I, and on that eminence is a
little pool said to be possessed of peculiar virtues.
To procure these virtues you must be a solitary
wanderer at sunrise, and if you wish to possess eternal
youth you must perform the acrobatic feat of getting
down head first between the shelving rocks, and kiss
the cool water of the pool just as the first rays of the
sun touch its dark brown waters.   They are many
who have made the pilgrimage to the Pool of Eternal
Youth, but whether they found what they went in
search of is another tale.

One night at dusk I lay just above this pool and
looked across the Isle of Dreams.   Beyond the Hill
of Noises, the cairn on the Carn-cul-ri-Eirinn was just

dimly visible, and this set me a-thinking. The sun had almost sunk behind the flat, sandy isle to the west in a glorious coloured haze. How long I lay there I do not know, for I must have fallen into a reverie. In my dreams I saw the fading radiance of the sunset on the distant horizon, and its reflected glory seemed to light up the dark crags all around me, and the Hill of Noises was bathed in purple light. In the softness of the afterglow, there gradually formed a wonderful corona which seemed floating in mid-air above the Port-a-Churaich. It threw a mellow golden light on the waters all around, and out of a dim mist which lay behind like a wisp of cumulus cloud, there appeared a little coracle made of the branches of trees and covered with skins. In it were thirteen men, and it drifted slowly in towards the pebbly beach of a little rocky bay which was once nameless, but which is now known as St. Columba's Bay.

The chill night air, and the roar of the surf on the Machair shore, roused me from my reverie. I found that twilight had given way to a soft velvety darkness which hung all around.

And so right down through the long days since Colum came, the sacred isle has been the home of dreams and will be so to all eternity.

> " We are such stuff
> As dreams are made on, and our little life
> Is rounded with a sleep."

EPILOGUE.

THE GRAIL-LIT ISLE.

ISLES of the West, farewell !
The cloud wrack is gathering fast in a dull and leaden sky. A chill and swithering wind blows in from the skerries, ruffling the feathers of the grey geese gathered on the machair ere they take their long flight to the winter feeding grounds.

The deer have been driven from their royal homes on the high hills by stress of weather. They are now on the lower slopes and in the valleys, feeding on soft grasses where yet the snow has not fallen. Wraith-like mists are creeping up the corries, and the high tops are enshrouded in virgin white. Most of the sea birds have deserted their summer haunts, and the quack of the wild duck is heard no more by the lone tarn-side.

Yesterday the lyre strings of summer were tuned and pouring forth sweet music. To-day there is only a lingering echo creeping down the glen and among the rocks of the wild seashore.

*   *   *   *   *   *

But although winter is upon us, the sun still shines on one fair isle—the elusive Tir-nan-Og, Land of Eternal Youth, of Beauty, and the Heart's Desire. Homeland of the Gael, no mortal isle art thou, subject to the tyranny of the seasons. On thee, enchanted island, it is ever spring, and spring is ever in the hearts of those who seek thy golden shores. They may dwell perforce amid the turmoil of the city, but their hearts respond to the wild, sweet call of Tir-nan-Og.

INDEX

A SELECTED LIST OF BOOKS
PRINCIPALLY RELATING TO
SCOTLAND

ENEAS MACKAY, STIRLING, SCOTLAND

The Wolfe of Badenoch. By Sir Thomas Dick Lauder. New Edition. 7/6 net. (post, 6d). A stirring romance of Scotland in the Fourteenth Century. With Foreword by R. B. Cunninghame Graham.

Human Voices. A collection of verse by G. R. Malloch. 2/6 net. (post, 2d).

Scotland : Picturesque and Traditional. By George Eyre-Todd. 5/- net. (post, 6d). Contains 384 pages and 56 illustrations.

Stirling : Twenty-one Drawings. By G. Elmslie Owen. Notes by David B. Morris. 3/6 net. (post, 4d). Charming Woodcut effects.

Scottish Diaries and Memoirs 1550-1746. Edited by J. G. Fyfe, M.A., with an Introduction by Professor R. S. Rait, C.B.E., LL.D., Historiographer Royal for Scotland. Fully Illustrated. 5/- net. (post, 6d.)

The Elusive Gael. By Dugald Coghill, with Introduction by the Duke of Sutherland. **Cr. 8vo.** 5/- net. (post, 4d.)

44 CRAIGS, STIRLING

A Highland Chapbook. By Isabel Cameron, the author of "The Doctor." Cr. 8vo. 3/6 net. (post, 4d.)

Smuggling in the Highlands. An account of Highland Whisky Smuggling Stories and Detections. By Ian MacDonald, I.S.O. With Illustrations of Smuggling Boothies, Distilling Utensils, etc. Post 8vo. 3s. (post, 4d.)

Who's Who in Burns. By J. D. Ross, LL.D. Containing over 600 references and cross references, and specially designed map. 10/6 net. (post, 6d.)

A Little Book of Burns Lore. By J. D. Ross, LL.D. With a Preface by James D. Law, author of "Dreams o' Hame." Crown 8vo. 3s. 6d. net. (post, 4d.)

Robert Burns and his Rhyming Friends. By J. D. Ross. With Notes by Geo. F. Black. Demy 8vo. 3s 6d net. (post, 6d).

Strange Tales of the Western Isles. By Halbert J. Boyd. 7/6 net. (post, 6d.) Nine weird and exciting tales.

Feuds of the Clans. By the Rev. Alexander MacGregor, M.A. Together with the History of the Feuds and Conflicts among the Clans in the Northern parts of Scotland and in the Western Isles. Crown 8vo. 3s. 6d. (post, 4d.)

Place Names of the Highlands and Islands of Scotland. By Alexander MacBain, M.A., LL.D. With Notes and Foreword by William Watson, M.A., LL.D. Demy 8vo. 21s. (post, 6d.)

Culloden Moor, and the Story of the Battle. With Description of the Stone Circles and Cairns at Clava. By the late Peter Anderson, of Inverness. Post 8vo. 5s. (post, 4d.)

Highland Superstitions. By Alexander MacGregor F.S.A. New Edition, with Introductory Chapter upon Superstitions and their Origin by Isabel Cameron. Demy 8vo. Gilt top. 3s. 6d. (post, 3d.)

Celtic Mythology and Religion. By Alexander MacBain. With Chapter upon Druid Circles and Celtic Burial, with Introductory Chapter and Notes by Professor W. J. Watson. Demy 8vo. 7s. 6d. (post, 6d.)

Gaelic Proverbs and Proverbial Sayings, with English Translations. By T. D. MacDonald. Crown 8vo. 5s. net. (postage, 6d.)

The Lake of Menteith : Its Islands and Vicinity. With Historical Accounts of the Priory of Inchmahome and Earldom of Menteith. By A. F. Hutchison. 15s. (post, 1s.)

Songs of the Gael (Gaelic and English). A collection in Sol-fa and Staff Notations. Paper edition, 1s.

The Romance of Poaching in the Highlands of Scotland. As illustrated in the Lives of John Farquharson and Alexander Davidson, the last of the Free Foresters. By W. M'Combie Smith. Crown 8vo. 3s. 6d. (post, 4d.)

Antiquarian Notes : A Series of Papers Regarding Families and Places in the Highlands. By Charles Fraser-MacKintosh of Drummond, F.S.A. Scot. 2nd Edition with the Life of the Author by Kenneth MacDonald. 21s. net. (post, 2d.)

The Prophecies of the Brahan Seer. By Alexander Mackenzie, F.S.A. Scot. With introductory Chapter by Andrew Lang. Demy 8vo. 3s. 6d. net. (postage, 4d.)

The Misty Isle of Skye : Its Scenery, Its People, Its Story. By J. A. MacCulloch. New and Revised Edition. With Introduction by MacLeod of MacLeod, C.M.G. Crown 8vo., 336 pp., 24 Half-tone Plates, and specially designed Map. 5s. net. (post, 6d.)

The Priory of Inchmahome : The Playground of Mary Queen of Scots. By A. A. Fitz-Allan. Fully Illustrated. 1s. 6d. net.

The Literature of the Highlanders. By Nigel MacNeill. New Edition. Edited and revised by J. MacMaster Campbell. 7/6 net. (post, 6d.)

Robert Louis Stevenson and the Scottish Highlanders. By David B. Morris. Cr. 8vo., 5/- (post, 6d).

Stirling Castle : Its place in Scottish History. By Eric Stair-Kerr. Introduction by The Earl of Mar and Kellie, and a Chapter on the Recent Excavations by J. S. Richardson. Fully Illustrated. 3s 6d (post, 6d).

BY MOUNTAIN
MOOR AND LOCH
TO THE
DREAM ISLES OF THE WEST